COLORADO BUCKET LIST

Set Off on **150 Epic Adventures** and Discover Incredible Destinations to Live Out Your Dreams While Creating Unforgettable Memories that Will Last a Lifetime.

(Online Digital MAP included - access it through the link provided in the MAP Chapter of this book)

BeCrePress Travel

TABLE OF CONTENTS

COLORADO BUCKET LIST

COLORADO BUCKET LIST

INTRODUCTION

Ready to shake up your ordinary, sit-at-home life? Fasten your seatbelts, because "Colorado Bucket List: Set Off on 150 Epic Adventures" is about to blast you off into the dazzling universe of Colorado's landscapes and cultural vibes. Trust me, this isn't the run-of-the-mill travel guide that lulls you to sleep; it's the cherry-on-top companion that promises a joyride like no other, helping you create memories that'll be cherished more than your grandma's secret apple pie recipe.

Ever had 150 jaw-dropping spots crammed into one roller-coaster ride of a book? Welcome aboard, my friend! This guide's going to serve up the natural splendor and diversity of Colorado on a silver platter. Imagine staring up at the mighty peaks of the Rockies that tower over you like an ancient titan, or exploring the mystical cliff dwellings of Mesa Verde that seem like they've popped straight out of a history book. Fancy a dance with Denver's lively streets? Or maybe a meditative stroll through the zen-like calm of the Great Sand Dunes National Park? Prepare to crisscross the Centennial State like a hummingbird on caffeine!

And no, we're not letting you dive in blindfolded. Each destination comes decked out with every tiny detail you'd need, curated with the precision of a Swiss watch. Addresses, nearby cities, driving directions, the best times to pop in for a visit, access costs (no such thing as a free lunch, right?), GPS coordinates, and website details - it's all there. So whether you're an adrenaline junkie, a history nerd, or a culture vulture, this book's got everything under the Colorado sun.

Just when you think it can't get better, voila! The book flexes an interactive map, lovingly and meticulously crafted by the author. Say sayonara to the head-scratching confusion of traditional maps and frustratingly complicated apps. This is your effortless, digital compass that'll navigate you to each of the 150 epic adventures, ensuring a smooth-as-silk exploration of Colorado's wonders.

So, with "Colorado Bucket List: Set Off on 150 Epic Adventures," it's not just about gazing at Colorado; it's about inhaling it, living it, and making it a part of your own epic tale. The memories? They'll stick with you longer than a catchy tune. So buckle up and polish those hiking boots. Your unforgettable journey is just a page away. Ready to turn your daydreams into tangible, laughter-filled, awe-inspiring realities? What are you waiting for? As they say, adventure waits for no one, will you seize it?

ABOUT COLORADO

To access the Digital Map, please refer to the 'Map Chapter' in this book

Landscape of Colorado

Colorado's geography is a stunning mosaic of contrasting landscapes. To the west, the majestic Rocky Mountains dominate the skyline, with soaring peaks that attract outdoor enthusiasts and adventure seekers. These mountains include iconic summits like Longs Peak, Mount Evans, Pikes Peak, and the Spanish Peaks. Glacial lakes, cascading waterfalls, and picturesque alpine meadows further enhance the mountainous allure of Colorado.

Descending from the mountains, the state unfolds into expansive plains that stretch eastward. The Great Plains offers a contrast to the ruggedness of the mountains with vast grasslands and rolling hills. The plains are punctuated by buttes and canyons, adding a touch of drama to the otherwise open landscapes. Notable regions in the plains include the Colorado Eastern Plains and the fertile agricultural lands of the South Platte River Valley.

Further south, the terrain transitions into the high desert landscapes of the San Luis Valley, where the headwaters of the Rio Grande flow. This region is characterized by arid plains, rocky hills, and the mesmerizing Great Sand Dunes, which create a surreal desert-like environment. The juxtaposition of these diverse landscapes within a single state is a testament to Colorado's natural wonders.

Flora and Fauna of Colorado

Colorado's varied ecosystems harbor an abundance of flora and fauna, each adapted to thrive in its specific habitat. The alpine regions, above the treeline, are home to hardy alpine vegetation such as lichens, mosses, and wildflowers. As one descends into the subalpine and montane zones, forests of conifers dominate the landscape, including species like ponderosa pine, Douglas fir, and Engelmann spruce. These forests provide habitat for numerous animal species, including elk, mule deer, black bears, and mountain lions.

The plains of Colorado are adorned with prairie grasses, offering sustenance for herbivores like pronghorn antelope and bison. Burrowing owls, prairie falcons, and meadowlarks grace the skies, while coyotes, prairie dogs, and swift foxes roam the grasslands. Riparian areas provide vital habitats for beavers, otters, and a variety of bird species.

In the arid desert regions, desert flora like yuccas, agaves, and cacti thrive, showcasing their resilience in the harsh environment. Wildlife in these arid landscapes includes desert bighorn sheep, rattlesnakes, and various species of lizards and rodents.

Climate of Colorado

Colorado's climate is influenced by its diverse geography and elevation changes. The state experiences four distinct seasons, each characterized by unique weather patterns. In general, Colorado's climate can be divided into three main regions: the eastern plains, the mountains, and the western slope.

The eastern plains have a semi-arid climate, with hot summers and cold winters. Thunderstorms are common during the summer months, providing relief from the heat and occasionally producing hail and tornadoes. The mountainous regions of Colorado offer cooler temperatures, with mild and pleasant summers and cold, snowy winters. The higher peaks of the Rockies receive abundant snowfall, making them a haven for winter sports enthusiasts.

The Western Slope has a variety of climates, from alpine climates in the highest elevations to desert-like conditions in the lower valleys. The region is influenced by the Colorado River and its tributaries, offering diverse habitats for wildlife and a range of recreational activities.

History of Colorado

The captivating history of Colorado unfolds like a tapestry, woven with threads of human habitation, exploration, and development spanning countless centuries. Through the ages, this remarkable state has witnessed the rise and fall of civilizations, from the ancient Pueblo peoples who left an indelible mark with their profound heritage, to the intrepid Spanish adventurers who claimed this land for themselves in the 16th century. The allure of Colorado stretches beyond imagination, where the wild west echoes with the tales of gold rushes and the courageous spirit of settlers who sought new horizons.

Colorado, affectionately known as the Centennial State, embodies a captivating fusion of diverse cultures and landscapes, providing a fertile ground for multiple civilizations to flourish. The Pueblo people, tracing their roots back a millennium, graced this region with their remarkable presence. They constructed awe-inspiring cliff dwellings, cunningly engineered irrigation systems, and cultivated bounteous crops such as maize and squash. Their vibrant communities, nestled near rivers and streams, thrived with life and meaning. Their spiritual practices and intricate belief systems, cherished still by their descendants, emanate a powerful aura that embraces the heart of this ancestral land.

In the annals of Colorado's chronicles, the year 1598 marks a turning point, as the valiant Don Juan de Oñate embarked on a mission of exploration and colonization. Leading a courageous entourage of 700 soldiers and settlers from Mexico, Oñate etched his name in history by erecting the first permanent settlement in Colorado, San Luis de la Culebra, in 1605. This pivotal moment heralded an era of Spanish influence that left an indelible imprint on Colorado's culture, architecture, and place names—it weaves a tapestry that still thrills the senses today.

The destiny of Colorado was further intertwined with the grand tapestry of American history in 1803 when it became a cherished part of the grand Louisiana Purchase. This monumental agreement between France and the United States ignited the flames of hope and possibility. American settlers, eager to unleash their dreams upon this newfound land, seized the opportunity to build a future unlike any other. As the pages of time turned, Colorado emerged as a state of its own, igniting the spirit of independence and resilience, and officially joining the Union in 1876.

Colorado's rich natural resources also played an important role in the development of the state. The discovery of gold in several regions during the mid-1800s led to a large influx of settlers hoping to make their fortunes. Gold rushes changed the economy and population growth of Colorado greatly, as mining towns sprung up all over the area. As more and more people moved to Colorado, trade routes were created between the east and west coasts of the United States—making it an important transportation hub for the country by the 1880s.

During World War II, Colorado faced several economic difficulties but experienced a boom after the 1970s when oil discoveries were made in the Eastern Plains region and the energy industry started to flourish again. This allowed for the development of several cities, such as Denver which is now a major business center for many industries today.

Colorado is also well known for its diverse cultural heritage which includes contributions from Native American tribes, Spanish colonizers, and miners. Today, Colorado offers visitors the chance to explore unique cultures from different time periods in history—from the ancient Puebloan civilizations to more modern gold rush settlements.

Tourism has become one of Colorado's most important industries in recent years due to its picturesque landscape, outdoor activities, and places of interest. With this book as your guide, you can explore some of the best destinations in Colorado and create your own unforgettable experiences!

I hope you enjoy your journey through this beautiful region as you discover all the hidden gems the Centennial State has to offer!

ASPEN

Maroon Bells

Find adventure and beauty in one of Colorado's most popular outdoor destinations, the iconic Maroon Bells. Nestled in the Rocky Mountains near Aspen, this stunningly picturesque area features two majestic 14er peaks - North & South Maroon Peak - surrounded by pine forests, meadows adorned with wildflowers, and lake-strewn valleys. Enjoy a hike along the exhilarating 10-mile (round trip) loop trail that winds around the mountains for an unforgettable experience, or take things slow and explore on horseback or mountain bike for a different perspective.

Location: Maroon-Snowmass Trail, Aspen, CO 81611 United States

Closest City or Town: Aspen, Colorado

How to Get There: Take Hwy 82 E from downtown Aspen for approximately 20 miles until you reach the trailhead parking lot on your left side.

GPS Coordinates: 39.0969465° N, 106.9470154° W

Best Time to Visit: Summer and fall months offer the best conditions for exploring comfortably.

Pass/Permit/Fees: There is no entrance fee, but permits are required in certain areas of the park. Please visit their website for more details.

Did you Know? The Maroon Bells are widely considered one of the most photographed mountains in North America!

Website: https://aspenchamber.org/plan-trip/trip-highlights/maroon-bells

Independence Pass

Explore an alpine wonderland when you visit Independence Pass, a stunningly beautiful 12,095-foot mountain pass in Colorado's Rocky Mountains. Take a drive along the gorgeous highway, stopping for breathtaking views of the Continental Divide and vibrant wildflower meadows. Look out for wildlife including elk, deer, moose, hawks, and bald eagles as you make your way through one of America's most scenic drives.

Location: Hwy 82, 20 miles E of Aspen, Aspen, CO 81611

Closest City or Town: Aspen, Colorado

How to Get There: From downtown Aspen take Highway 82 East until you reach the summit at mile marker 56.

GPS Coordinates: 39.1793413° N, 106.8020296° W

Best Time to Visit: Summer months are best for taking in the breathtaking views along the highway.

Pass/Permit/Fees: There is no entrance fee, but permits are required for certain activities. Please visit their website for more details.

Did you Know? The Pass is named after a group of settlers who traveled west to settle in California in 1846!

Website: http://www.independencepass.org/

The John Denver Sanctuary

Get a taste of Colorado's famed folk singer and songwriter at The John Denver Sanctuary, located in Aspen's Rio Grande Park. This tranquil sanctuary honors the late musician with its gorgeous meadow setting and stunning mountain backdrop, offering a peaceful place to relax and reflect on his life and legacy. Visitors can take a stroll through the beautiful meadow and enjoy the vibrant wildflowers, before exploring the nearby John Denver Plaza which features sculptures inspired by his music.

Location: 470 Rio Grande Pl, Aspen, CO 81611 United States

Closest City or Town: Aspen, Colorado

How to Get There: From Downtown Aspen head south on Spring St for 0.3 miles and turn right onto East Hyman Ave. Follow E Hyman Ave for 0.9 miles until you reach Rio Grande Park on your left side.

GPS Coordinates: 39.1925469° N, 106.81648° W

Best Time to Visit: Summer months offer the best conditions for enjoying outdoor activities in the park.

Pass/Permit/Fees: The Sanctuary is free and open to the public year-round.

Did you Know? The sanctuary also features an outdoor amphitheater that was used for one of John Denver's live performances in 1999!

Website: http://www.aspenrecreation.com/john-denver-sanctuary

T-Lazy-7 Ranch

Feel the Wild West come alive at T-Lazy-7 Ranch! Nestled in the White River National Forest near Aspen, Colorado, this ranch offers a unique glimpse into cowboy life. Take a ride through stunning mountain trails on horseback or explore on foot and immerse yourself in nature with breathtaking views of Maroon Bells. Enjoy western adventures like fly fishing, archery lessons, and campfires under the starry desert sky - it's an experience you won't forget!

Location: 3129 Maroon Creek Rd, Aspen CO 81611-3561

GPS Coordinates: 39.1669488° N, 106.8790774° W

Closest City or Town: Aspen Colorado (just outside city limits)

How to Get There: from downtown Aspen take Maroon Creek Road for 6 miles until you reach T Lazy 7 Ranch

Best Time to Visit: open year round but cooler months are better for outdoor activities

Pass/Permit/Fees: Vary depending on activity ($15-$60)

Did you Know? The main lodge was built in 1918 by Francis Whitaker and has been featured in several movies including City Slickers and An Unfinished Life

Website: http://tlazy7.com/

Aspen Mountain

Take your breath away with a visit to Aspen Mountain, located in the heart of the Rocky Mountains. From skiing down exhilarating slopes to snowshoeing through majestic forests, Aspen Mountain offers an unforgettable winter experience. During warmer months, enjoy breathtaking views from the summit while hiking or mountain biking. With spectacular scenery and endless outdoor activities, this majestic destination will have you coming back for more!

Location: Colorado 81611, United States

GPS Coordinates: 39.1116318° N, 106.8650395° W

Closest City or Town: Aspen, Colorado

How to Get There: take Highway 82 and turn left onto Aspen Mountain Road until you reach the base of the mountain

Best Time to Visit: Summer months for hiking & biking and Winter months for skiing & snowshoeing

Pass/Permit/Fees: Vary depending on activities ($20-$200)

Did you Know? Aspen Mountain was first opened in 1947 making it one of the original ski resorts in North America!

Website: http://www.aspensnowmass.com/aspen-mountain

Maroon Lake Scenic Trail

Take a journey into natural beauty with a visit to Maroon Lake Scenic Trail. located just outside Aspen, Colorado in the White River National Forest. Soak up breathtaking views of the Maroon Bells Mountains as you trek along this 8-mile loop trail. From fishing to wildlife spotting, there's something for everyone at this scenic destination - come marvel at the wonders of nature!

Location: 33X5+CP Aspen, Colorado, United States

GPS Coordinates: 39.0985625° N, 106.9406875° W

Closest City or Town: Aspen, Colorado

How to Get There: Take Highway 82 and turn left onto Maroon Creek Road until you reach the lake entrance

Best Time to Visit: Summer months are best for outdoor activities

Pass/Permit/Fees: Free admission to the trail

Did you Know? Maroon Lake Scenic Trail was voted one of America's most picturesque hikes!

Website: http://www.aspenchamber.org/explore-aspen/trip-highlights/maroon-bells

Silver Queen Gondola

Let your senses take flight with a scenic ride on the Silver Queen Gondola in Aspen, Colorado. Located behind Ajax Tavern, this gondola whisks you up to 11,212 feet above sea level for stunning views of downtown Aspen and the surrounding Rocky Mountains. The picturesque journey takes about 8 minutes each way and is perfect for sightseeing or catching one of nature's breathtaking sunsets.

Location: E Durant & S Hunter St (behind Ajax Tavern), Aspen, CO 81611

GPS Coordinates: 39.1865426° N, 106.8179095° W

Closest City or Town: Aspen, Colorado

How to Get There: Behind Ajax Tavern in downtown Aspen

Best Time to Visit: Summer months are best for taking advantage of warmer temperatures

Pass/Permit/Fees: Tickets range from $9-$21 depending on age **Did you Know?** On clear days you can see over 100 miles away!

Website: http://www.aspensnowmass.com/summer-recreation/gondola-and-lift-rides

Rio Grande Trail

Explore the great outdoors with an awe-inspiring ride along the Rio Grande Trail bike path in Central Colorado! This 43-mile trail follows a former railroad line that winds through dramatic mountain scenery as it passes through the communities of Aspen, Snowmass Village, Woody Creek, and Basalt. Enjoy peaceful nature hikes or take a leisurely ride on your bike - no matter what activity you choose, this beautiful trail is sure to leave you with amazing memories.

Location: 235 Puppy Smith St, Aspen, CO 81611

GPS Coordinates: 39.1937044° N, 106.8196142° W

Closest City or Town: Aspen, Colorado

How to Get There: From downtown Aspen head south on Monarch Street for 0.3 miles then turn left onto Puppy Smith Street

Best Time to Visit: Spring is best as temperatures are mild and the wildflowers in bloom

Pass/Permit/Fees: Free to use.

Did you Know? The trail is part of the larger Colorado Front Range Trail.

Website: https://www.rfta.com/trail-information/

Buttermilk Mountain

Glide down the slopes and let your senses come alive at Buttermilk Mountain! Located just outside of Aspen, this mountain offers 11 lifts and a full range of trails for skiers and snowboarders of all levels. Whether you're looking for beginner-friendly bunny slopes or challenging black diamonds, there's something here to suit everyone's needs! On top of that, take advantage of the mountain's lift-served terrain park and superpipe for a truly thrilling experience.

Location: 38700 Highway 82, Aspen, CO 81611

GPS Coordinates: 39.2058193° N, 106.8605805° W

Closest City or Town: Aspen, Colorado

How to Get There: From downtown Aspen take Highway 82 east for 5 miles then turn left onto Buttermilk Road

Best Time to Visit: Winter months offer the best snow conditions

Pass/Permit/Fees: Lift tickets range from $54-$179 depending on age

Did you Know? Buttermilk is one of four ski areas in the Aspen Snowmass resort area!

Website: http://www.aspensnowmass.com/our-mountains/buttermilk

BEAVER CREEK

Beaver Creek Ski Area

An excellent destination for thrill seekers and adventure lovers, Beaver Creek Ski Area in Colorado is the ideal spot for a winter retreat. With over 150 trails, ski and snowboard rentals, tubing hills, sleigh rides, Nordic skiing and so much more—this place has something to offer everyone. Whether you're looking to just take it easy or throw down some extreme stunts on the slopes – this is your go-to mountain resort!

Location: Beaver Creek Resort Blvd., Avon CO 81620

Closest City or Town: Beaver Creek, Colorado

How to Get There: From Eagle County Regional Airport head south on I-70 E towards Avon/Vail Exit 167. Turn left onto US-6 W/Exit 171 then turn right onto Cooley Mesa Road before turning right again onto West Beano's Boulevard to reach Beaver Creek Ski Area.

GPS Coordinates: 39.604225° N, 106.516515° W

Best Time to Visit: Winter months are best for skiing conditions but summer months are great too with plenty of activities available such as hiking and biking trails among others.

Pass/Permit/Fees: Entrance fees vary depending on the type of activities ($20-$50). Please visit their website for more details.

Did you Know? Beaver Creek Ski Area is home to the Birds of Prey World Cup, one of the most prestigious alpine ski events in the world!

Website: http://www.beavercreek.com/

BOULDER

Colorado Chautauqua: Park

Discover the beauty and natural wonders of Colorado Chautauqua: Park in Boulder. With its stunning mountain views and a variety of activities to choose from, this spot is perfect for those looking for an adventure! Hike or bike around the trails, explore unique rock formations at Flatirons Vista Trailhead, or take a dip in one of the many swimming holes. Don't forget to grab a bite at the Dining Hall or if you're up for it, take part in one of their special events like concerts and festivals.

Location: 900 Baseline Rd., Boulder, CO 80302-7547

Closest City or Town: Boulder, Colorado

How to Get There: From Denver International Airport take I-70 W towards Grand Junction. Take Exit 266 to merge onto US-36 E/Boulder Turnpike and follow it for 12 miles before exiting on CO 93 N and turning left onto Baseline Road.

GPS Coordinates: 40.000023° N, 105.2819456° W

Best Time to Visit: Summer months are the most popular time to visit Colorado Chautauqua: Park due to the mild temperatures and abundant activities.

Pass/Permit/Fees: Entrance fees vary depending on the type of activities ($6-$15). Please visit their website for more details.

Did you Know? Colorado Chautauqua offers a unique lodging experience, with wooden cabins set among lush grounds and breathtaking views from every angle!

Website: http://www.chautauqua.com/

Flatirons

Explore the majestic Flatirons in Boulder, Colorado, and be amazed by its soaring cliffs that have been formed over thousands of years of erosion! Whether you're looking for an easy trek or an advanced hike up one of the rocks—the Flatirons are the perfect place to get your heart racing. Take in stunning views of the Boulder Valley, see if you can spot a peregrine falcon, and enjoy a picnic at one of the many picturesque spots along the way.

Location: Boulder Mountain Park, Boulder CO 80302

Closest City or Town: Boulder, Colorado

How to Get There: From Denver International Airport take I-70 W towards Grand Junction. Take Exit 266 to merge onto US-36 E/Boulder Turnpike and follow it for 7 miles before exiting on Baseline Road and taking a right turn into Richmond Drive. Follow it until you reach Chautauqua Park Entrance A, where you can park and start your hike.

GPS Coordinates: 39.9990809° N, 105.2952959° W

Best Time to Visit: Spring and autumn months are the best times to visit Flatirons as temperatures are cooler, but summer months can be just as enjoyable with plenty of shade available from the trees.

Pass/Permit/Fees: Free!

Did you Know? The Boulder Valley is home to many species of birds and wildlife, so keep an eye out during your hike—you might just spot a bobcat or a grouse!

Website: https://www.bouldercoloradousa.com/things-to-do/insider-guides/flatirons/

Boulder Creek Path

Discover the beauty of Boulder, Colorado on a scenic stroll along the Boulder Creek Path. This 18-mile path parallels Arapahoe Avenue and meanders through urban parks, natural areas, and city streets as it makes its way from Boulder Canyon to Valmont Park. Enjoy panoramic views of nearby mountains while taking in the sights and sounds of your surroundings with every step. For an adventurous outdoor outing beyond just walking or biking, try rafting or tubing down the creek!

Location: Parallels Arapahoe Ave., Boulder, CO 80302

Closest City or Town: Located within the city limits of Boulder

How to Get There: From downtown Boulder follow either Canyon Blvd./Arapahoe Ave east until you reach Cherryvale Rd. Turn left onto Cherryvale Rd., then turn right once you reach N Broadway St./US-36

E/US-287 S/CO-119 S for about 2 miles until you see signs for access points to their park system.

GPS Coordinates: 40.0146719° N, 105.2379885° W

Best Time to Visit: During summer months when temperatures are milder

Pass/Permit/Fees: Free admission.

Did you Know? The Boulder Creek Path was one of the first paths established by the City of Boulder in the late 1970s!

Website: http://bouldercolorado.gov/parks-rec/boulder-creek-path

University of Colorado at Boulder

Explore one of America's most renowned universities, located in beautiful Boulder, Colorado. Founded in 1876, CU Boulder is home to a vibrant student body and awe-inspiring views of the Rocky Mountains. Take a self-guided tour to see highlights such as Norlin Quadrangle, Old Main, and Fiske Planetarium. Enjoy outdoor adventures like biking or hiking on trails near campus or take in a Rocky Mountain sunset atop the Flatirons.

Location: 2200 Colorado Ave, Boulder, CO 80309, United States

Closest City or Town: Located within the city limits of Boulder

How to Get There: From downtown Boulder follow Canyon Blvd./Arapahoe Ave east until you reach US-36 E/US-287 S/CO-119 S. Turn left onto US-36 E/US-287 S and then turn right onto Baseline Rd. Follow for about 3 miles until you reach Colorado Ave. Turn left onto Colorado Ave. and the University of Colorado at Boulder will be on your right.

GPS Coordinates: 40.0079667° N, 105.2658615° W

Best Time to Visit: Summer months are the best time for visiting as temperatures tend to be milder during that season

Pass/Permit/Fees: There is no charge to access the University of Colorado campus but visitors must follow all posted rules and regulations.

Did you Know? The University of Colorado is home to eight Nobel Laureates, including physicist Carl Von Weizsacker!

Website: http://www.colorado.edu/

Eldorado Canyon

Unlock a hidden gem in Boulder, Colorado, and embark on an outdoor adventure at Eldorado Canyon State Park. Located just outside of Boulder, this park offers breathtaking views of rugged red rock canyons formed by the South Platte River. Explore stunning hiking trails, rock-climb routes for all levels, and a variety of other activities like camping, fishing, biking, and more. An added bonus is seeing the historic railroad tunnel near the park entrance!

Location: 321 Eldorado Springs Dr, Boulder, CO 80303 United States

Closest City or Town: Located outside of Boulder

How to Get There: From downtown Boulder follow either Canyon Blvd./Arapahoe Ave east until you reach Cherryvale Rd. Turn left onto Cherryvale Rd., then turn right once you reach N Broadway St./US-36 E/US-287 S/CO-119 S for about 11 miles until you see signs for access points to Eldorado Canyon State Park.

GPS Coordinates: 39.931811° N, 105.2799992° W

Best Time to Visit: Spring and Fall are the best times to visit as temperatures tend to be milder in those seasons.

Pass/Permit/Fees: There is a $8 per car fee for daily access or $55 for an annual pass.

Did you Know? The area around Eldorado Canyon was home to the Arapaho Native American tribe for thousands of years before settlers arrived!

Website: http://www.colorado.com/cities-and-towns/eldorado-springs

Flagstaff Mountain

This is a must-visit spot for outdoor enthusiasts! Take in breathtaking views of the Rocky Mountains from the top of Flagstaff Mountain, located just west of Boulder, Colorado. Hike up or take the free shuttle to reach this popular lookout point and enjoy trails for all levels. Bring your camera and snap some Instagram-worthy photos as you explore this incredible alpine environment.

Location: 2M3W+FJ Boulder, Colorado, United States

Closest City or Town: Boulder, Colorado

How to Get There: From downtown Boulder head along US-36 W towards Arapahoe Ave for 4 miles before turning right onto Baseline Rd. Turn left at 3rd St., then left again onto Flagstaff Road until you can go no further—the trailhead is straight ahead.

GPS Coordinates: 40.0036875° N, 105.3034375° W

Best Time to Visit: Spring and fall are the best times to visit when temperatures are milder and snow has melted away

Pass/Permit/Fees: The park is free year-round unless otherwise indicated by event signs onsite

Did you Know? Flagstaff Mountain offers one of the best views in Boulder—on a clear day, you can even see all the way to Denver!

Website: http://bouldercolorado.gov/osmp/flagstaff-trailhead

BRECKENRIDGE

Breckenridge Gondola

Go big or go home! Get high above Breckenridge and take an unforgettable ride on the Breckenridge Gondola. This exciting 8-minute journey will transport you from the base of Peak 9 to 12,000 feet up in the sky for some incredible panoramic mountain views along the way. Plus, with several restaurants located at the summit, there is plenty to explore once you get there!

Location: 170 Watson Avenue, Breckenridge, CO 80424, United States

Closest City or Town: Breckenridge, Colorado

How to Get There: From downtown Breckenridge take N Main St. until you reach Watson Ave. Turn right onto Watson, then turn left into the parking lot just past Ski Hill Rd.

GPS Coordinates: 39.4853101° N, 106.0478073° W

Best Time to Visit: Summer and winter months offer great visibility and warm temperatures

Pass/Permit/Fees: Tickets are required for riding the gondola ($25+) and can be purchased at the ticket office onsite

Did you Know? The Breckenridge Gondola is one of the highest-elevation gondolas in the US?

Website: http://www.breckenridgeresortmanagers.com/37/breck

Main Street

Explore downtown Breckenridge on foot! Historical buildings, unique shops, and delicious restaurants line Main Street—a colorful display of local culture that is perfect for a leisurely stroll or weekend getaway. Popular activities include visiting notable landmarks like the Barney Ford House Museum or enjoying some live music at one of Main Street's many bars and breweries.

Location: 137 S Main St, Breckenridge, CO 80424, United States

Closest City or Town: Breckenridge, Colorado

How to Get There: From the Breckenridge Gondola take Ski Hill Rd. to Main St., then turn left and make your way south until you reach 137 S Main St.

GPS Coordinates: 39.4807751° N, 106.0464297° W

Best Time to Visit: Anytime during summer or winter months when temperatures are milder

Pass/Permit/Fees: Access to Main Street is free year-round unless otherwise indicated by event signs onsite

Did you Know? The first telephone in Breckenridge was installed at a saloon on Main Street in 1881!

Website: http://www.gobreck.com/

McCullough Gulch

Experience a unique adventure at McCullough Gulch. Nestled in the White River National Forest, this scenic trail offers amazing views of cascading waterfalls and lush wildflowers in the summer months. With its dramatic landscape, this spot is perfect for hiking, wildlife watching, and photography. Its remote location also makes it an ideal place to camp under the starry desert sky!

Location: 82 Co Rd 850, Breckenridge CO 80424 United States

Closest City or Town: Breckenridge Colorado

How to Get There: From downtown Breckenridge take I-70 W towards Silverthorne. Take exit 205 and turn left onto US-6/CO-9 E which will lead you onto US-6N/BLUE RIVER PKWY S. Turn right on CO Rd 851 (Gore Creek Dr), then left on Co Rd 850 N to reach your destination.

GPS Coordinates: 39.3823818° N, 106.0643164° W

Best Time to Visit: Spring is the best time for visiting as temperatures tend to be milder during that season

Pass/Permit/Fees: Entrance to McCullough Gulch is free

Did you Know? This area was once a gold-mining camp and the site of an old toll bridge, which gave it its name.

Website:https://www.fs.usda.gov/recarea/whiteriver/recreation/recarea/?recid=40643&actid=50

CANON CITY

Royal Gorge Bridge and Park

Take your breath away at Royal Gorge Bridge and Park, one of Colorado's most impressive attractions. Situated in Cañon City on the edge of the Arkansas River, this location is home to a suspension bridge that towers above the canyon at 1,260 feet tall! Take in the stunning views of the towering cliffs as you wander down the paths and ride one of the world's highest aerial tramway. For an unforgettable experience, traverse across the bridge for a closer look!

Location: 4218 County Road 3a, Canon City, CO 81212-3663

Closest City or Town: Cañon City, Colorado

How to Get There: From downtown Cañon City take US-50 W until you reach Royer Rd. Turn left onto Co Rd 3A/Royal Gorge Bridge Rd., then follow it until you see signs for Royal Gorge Bridge Park entrance.

GPS Coordinates: 38.4621245° N, 105.3245132° W

Best Time to Visit: Summer months are the best time for visiting as temperatures tend to be milder during that season

Pass/Permit/Fees: Entrance fees vary depending on activities ($20-$28). Please visit their website for more details.

Did you Know? The Royal Gorge Bridge is the highest suspension bridge in North America and the second-highest in the world!

Website: https://royalgorgebridge.com/

Skyline Drive

Embark on an unforgettable drive at Skyline Drive, located in Cañon City, Colorado. This winding road stretches 5 miles along the top of a cliff with incredible views of the Arkansas River below and landmarks such as Mount Pisgah and Fish Hatchery Peak above. Park your car and explore the trails for a closer look at the stunning scenery or take in the views from one of the many scenic overlooks.

Location: Cañon City, Colorado 81212 United States

Closest City or Town: Cañon City, Colorado

How to Get There: From downtown Cañon City take US-50 W until you reach Royer Rd. Turn left onto Co Rd 3A/Royal Gorge Bridge Rd., then turn right on Skyline Drive to reach your destination.

GPS Coordinates: 38.4494063° N, 105.2253316° W

Best Time to Visit: Mid-Spring to early Fall is the best time for visiting as temperatures tend to be milder during that season

Pass/Permit/Fees: Skyline Drive is free of charge.

Did you Know? The breathtaking views from this drive are often compared to those of the Grand Canyon!

Website: http://www.canoncity.org/visitors/skyline_drive.php

CASCADE

Pikes Peak - America's Mountain

Discover breathtaking views of the Rocky Mountains at Pikes Peak – America's Mountain! Located in Cascade, Colorado, this majestic 14,114-foot summit is one of the most iconic natural landmarks in the United States. Take a drive up to the top for sweeping panoramas and explore accessible trails where you can spot soaring bald eagles or wildflowers. For an unforgettable experience, join a guided tour that includes lunch and lessons about local history and ecology.

Location: 5089 Pikes Peak Hwy, Cascade, CO 80809

Closest City or Town: Cascade

How to Get There: Head west on Highway 24 from Colorado Springs/Manitou Springs until you reach US-24 W Ramp (Exit 141A). Follow it towards Divot Rd., then turn right onto Pikes Peak Hwy to reach your destination.

GPS Coordinates: 38.9085673° N, 104.9827364° W

Best Time to Visit: The park is open year-round but mid-June through August offers milder temperatures while late September through November gives visitors stunning fall colors as well as fewer crowds

Pass/Permit/Fees: Fees vary depending on activities

Did you Know? The summit was featured in the famous song "America the Beautiful" written by Katharine Lee Bates in 1893.

Website: http://www.pikespeakcolorado.com/

North Pole - Santa's Workshop

Take a magical journey to the North Pole with Santa and his elves! Located in Cascade, Colorado, Santa's Workshop offers fun-filled days of Christmas-themed activities for the whole family to enjoy. Tour Santa's house, meet the reindeer and hop on a ride of your choice. With festive seasonal decorations, caroling elves, and other surprises around every corner, it truly feels like you're at the North Pole!

Location: 5050 Pikes Peak Hwy, Cascade, CO 80809-1123

Closest City or Town: Cascade

How to Get There: Take US-24 W Ramp (Exit 141A), then onto Divot Rd. Turn right onto Pikes Peak Hwy and you will soon reach your destination.

GPS Coordinates: 38.9049434° N, 104.9773563° W

Best Time to Visit: The park is open year-round but the best time to visit would be from late November to early December for Christmas-themed activities

Pass/Permit/Fees: Fees vary depending on activities

Did you Know? Santa's Workshop first opened in 1956, making it one of the oldest theme parks in Colorado.

Website: http://northpolecolorado.com/

CENTRAL CITY

Hidee Gold Mine

Take a trip back in time and experience the gold rush of Central City! Hidee Gold Mine is located in Central City, Colorado, and offers tours of an authentic underground gold mine. Learn about the history and geology of the area from experienced miners while taking part in hands-on activities like panning for gold and gemstones.

Location: 1950 Hidee Mine Rd. MM 6.3 Central City Parkway, Central City, CO 80427

Closest City or Town: Central City

How to Get There: Take US Route 6 West from Boulder/Denver until you reach the Central City exit. Turn left on State Highway 119 and follow it until you reach Central City Parkway. Take a right onto Hidee Mine Rd to get to your destination.

GPS Coordinates: 39.7888022° N, 105.4987377° W

Best Time to Visit: The park is open year-round but mid-June through August offers milder temperatures while late September through November gives visitors stunning fall colors as well as fewer crowds.

Pass/Permit/Fees: Fees vary depending on activities

Did you Know? Hidee Gold Mine is one of the oldest mines in Colorado, having been operational since 1859.

Website: http://www.hideegoldmine.com/

CHIMNEY ROCK

Chimney Rock National Monument

At Chimney Rock National Monument, explore the stunning views of southwestern Colorado overlooking San Juan National Forest. Walk through mysterious passages dedicated to ancestral Puebloans and discover artifacts from over 1,000 years ago. Climb up into the sky tower for a breathtaking view of the area or take one of the guided tours around the monument. At this marvel of history and culture, you'll never run out of things to do!

Location: 3179 Co-151, Chimney Rock, CO 81121

Closest City or Town: Durango, Colorado (approximately an hour's drive away)

How to Get There: Take US-160 E towards Pagosa Springs until you reach Mt Mestas Rd/Co Rd 151 in Archuleta County. Turn right onto Co Rd 151 until you reach Chimney Rock National Monument entrance Road on your left side.

GPS Coordinates: 37.1750699° N, 107.3031922° W

Best Time to Visit: The park is open year-round but summer months are the best time for exploring since it offers mild temperatures with clear skies during that period

Pass/Permit/Fees: Entrance fees vary depending on activities ($5-$15). Please visit their website for more details.

Did you Know? Chimney Rock National Monument was designated a World Heritage Site in 1970 due to its significance in the history and culture of the southwestern United States.

Website:http://www.fs.usda.gov/detail/sanjuan/specialplaces/?cid =stelprdb5390324

COLORADO SPRINGS

Garden of the Gods

Immerse yourself in a natural wonderland at Garden of the Gods, located in Colorado Springs, Colorado. This magnificent park features stunning red rock formations and sandstone cliffs that tower over 300 feet high. Take a hike around the area and explore the various trails or take a horseback riding tour to get the best views of this amazing place. Enjoy spectacular sunsets with friends or family and create lasting memories that you won't forget!

Location: 1805 N 30th St, Colorado Springs, CO 80904,

Closest City or Town: Colorado Springs, Colorado (a short drive away)

How to Get There: From downtown Colorado Springs take US-24 W until you reach N 30th St. Turn left and follow the signs for the Garden of the Gods entrance.

GPS Coordinates: 38.8783986° N, 104.8697704° W

Best Time to Visit: The park is open year-round but summer months are the best time for visiting as temperatures tend to be milder during that season

Pass/Permit/Fees: Entrance fees vary depending on activities ($5-$30). Please visit their website for more details.

Did you Know? Garden of the Gods is Colorado's oldest State Park, which was declared a National Natural Landmark in 1971 due to its unique geological features and stunning landscape.

Website: http://www.gardenofgods.com/

Cheyenne Mountain Zoo

Experience the wonder of wildlife at Cheyenne Mountain Zoo, one of the most acclaimed zoos in the United States! This unique zoo is located at 6,800 feet above sea level on Cheyenne Mountain overlooking Colorado Springs, making it one of the highest zoological parks in the world. Enjoy up-close encounters with animals like giraffes and tigers as you wander around the immaculately kept grounds.

With a focus on conservation and education, this is sure to be an unforgettable experience for visitors of all ages!

Location: 4250 Cheyenne Mountain Zoo Rd, Colorado Springs, CO 80906-5755

Closest City or Town: Colorado Springs, Colorado (a short drive away)

How to Get There: From downtown Colorado Springs take US-24 W until you reach Cheyenne Mountain Zoo Rd. Turn left and follow the signs for the zoo entrance.

GPS Coordinates: 38.7703821° N, 104.8550161° W

Best Time to Visit: The zoo is open year-round but summer months are best as temperatures tend to be milder during that season

Pass/Permit/Fees: Entrance fees vary depending on activities ($5-$20). Please visit their website for more details.

Did you Know? Cheyenne Mountain Zoo is the only Zoological Park in the world to have Giant Underground Aquarium Tunnels!

Website: http://www.cmzoo.org/

United States Air Force Academy

Experience the grandeur of the United States Air Force Academy in Colorado Springs, a setting steeped in history. Tour the iconic grounds and explore the stunning architecture and monuments, including the signature chapel. Watch as cadets train and take part in sports activities, and admire one of America's most prestigious military academies from up close. A visit to this Academy is unforgettable!

Location: 4102 Pinion Dr, Colorado Springs, CO 80840-2502

Closest City or Town: Colorado Springs

How to Get There: From Downtown Colorado Springs head south on W Vermijo Avenue toward S Tejon Street then turn right onto US-24W until you reach 31st St/Hwy 24 Turn left onto 31st street and drive for about 2 miles until you see signs for U.S air force academy Entrance at Pinion Drive

GPS Coordinates: 38.9916448° N, 104.8846858° W

Best Time to Visit: Summer months are the best time for visiting as temperatures tend to be milder during that season

Pass/Permit/Fees: Admission is free but visitors must register online before entering.

Did you Know? The United States Air Force Academy was founded in 1954 and has graduated over 80,000 cadets since then.

Website: http://www.academyadmissions.com/visit-the-academy/

National Museum of World War II Aviation

Step back in time at the National Museum of World War II Aviation located in Colorado Springs. Marvel at over 30 restored vintage aircraft from the era, including iconic fighters such as the P-51 Mustang and B-17 Flying Fortress. Learn about aviation history through interactive exhibits and talks given by veterans at this amazing museum!

Location: 775 Aviation Way, Colorado Springs, CO 80916-2740

Closest City or Town: Colorado Springs

How to Get There: From Downtown Colorado Springs head south on W Vermijo Avenue toward S Tejon Street then turn right onto US-24W until you reach Aviation Way. Turn left onto Aviation Way and the museum will be on your right.

GPS Coordinates: 38.8213693° N, 104.7201947° W

Best Time to Visit: Summer months are the best time for visiting as temperatures tend to be milder during that season

Pass/Permit/Fees: Entrance fees vary depending on activities ($5-$20). Please visit their website for more details.

Did you Know? The National Museum of World War II Aviation is one of the largest collections of original WWII aircraft in the United States!

Website: http://www.worldwariiaviation.org/

Red Rock Canyon

Discover a stunning oasis of beauty and history at Red Rock Canyon located south of U.S. 24 near the 31st St. base of Pikes Peak, Colorado Springs. This spectacular park provides breathtaking scenery, including its unique sandstone formations that remind us of its ancient origins as an ocean floor millions of years ago. Adventure seekers can enjoy hiking and mountain biking along scenic trails, while nature lovers can take part in guided tours or simply observe the abundant wildlife from a quiet spot by the canyon wall!

Location: south of U.S. 24 near 31st St. base of Pikes Peak, Colorado Springs, CO 80904

Closest City or Town: Colorado Springs

How to Get There: From Downtown Colorado Springs head south on W Vermijo Avenue toward S Tejon Street then turn right onto US-24W until you reach 31st St/Hwy 24 Turn left onto 31st street and drive for about 2 miles until you see signs for Red Rock Canyon entrance.

GPS Coordinates: 38.8539815° N, 104.8716628° W

Best Time to Visit: Summer months are the best time for visiting as temperatures tend to be milder during that season

Pass/Permit/Fees: Admission is free.

Did you Know? Red Rock Canyon is a popular destination for rock climbing and bouldering due to its unique sandstone formations!

Website: http://www.redrockcanyonopenspace.org/

Glen Eyrie Castle

Gain a sense of enchantment as you explore the ancient architecture and lush gardens of Glen Eyrie Castle in Colorado Springs. Seated on top of a picturesque hill, this residential castle offers breathtaking views from the balcony and plenty to discover inside. Take a guided tour to learn about the history of how it was built in the late 19th century, or browse through its collections of art and literature. Afterward, visit one of their many shops for souvenirs like antiques, tea sets, crystal jewelry, and more!

Location: 3820 N 30th St., Colorado Springs CO 80904-5001

Closest City or Town: Situated within Colorado Springs

How to Get There: From downtown take Interstate 25 until you reach exit 147/Circle Drive. Head east on Circle Dr., then turn right onto Garden Of The Gods Rd., then left onto W Rockrimmon Blvd. Finally turn right onto N 30th St., where you will find the castle at number 3820.

GPS Coordinates: 38.8917006° N, 104.8754256° W

Best Time to Visit: Open year-round (except for major holidays), but summer months are best to explore the castle grounds.

Pass/Permit/Fees: Prices may vary but are generally $17 for adults and $10 for children (ages 5-12).

Did you Know? Glen Eyrie Castle was built by legendary railroad magnate, General William Jackson Palmer, who also co-founded Colorado Springs.

Website: http://www.gleneyrie.org/

Cosmo's Magic Theater

Be amazed at the extraordinary illusions and magic tricks from master illusionist Cosmo's 'The Magnificent' at his eponymous theater in Garden Of The Gods Plaza. See showstopping performances that will leave you speechless as well as audience participation opportunities where you can get up close and personal with Cosmo himself. After the show, don't forget to visit his onsite museum for a chance to see some of his original props and costumes!

Location: 1045 Garden of the Gods Rd Suite I, Colorado Springs, CO 80907

Closest City or Town: Situated within Colorado Springs

How to Get There: From downtown take Interstate 25 until you reach exit 146/Garden Of The Gods Rd. Head eastbound on Garden Of The Gods Rd., then turn right onto N 30th St which will bring you straight into the Plaza where you can find Cosmo's Theater at unit 1045.

GPS Coordinates: 38.8961524° N, 104.8421783° W

Best Time to Visit: Shows are scheduled throughout the year so there's no bad time to visit!

Pass/Permit/Fees: Tickets typically cost between $14 and $20. Please check their website for details and more information on upcoming shows.

Did you Know? Cosmo has been performing magic professionally since 1975, making him one of the most experienced illusionists in the world!

Website: http://www.cosmosmagictheater.com/calendar

North Cheyenne Cañon Park & Starsmore Discovery Center

Unlock the mysteries of nature at North Cheyenne Cañon Park and its adjacent Starsmore Discovery Center - a perfect place for nature lovers to explore in Colorado Springs. Hike or bike along its scenic trails, camp under the starry desert sky, or just enjoy a picnic with family and friends. Don't forget to visit the Discovery Center for interactive exhibits on the area's flora and fauna as well as astronomy programs that take place each month!

Location: 2120 S Cheyenne Canon Rd, Colorado Springs, CO 80906

Closest City or Town: Situated within Colorado Springs

How to Get There: From downtown take Interstate 25 until you reach exit 143/Garden Of The Gods Rd., then turn westbound onto Garden Of The Gods Rd., followed by a right onto N Cheyenne Cañon Rd. which will bring you straight into the Park.

How to Get There: From downtown take Interstate 25 until you reach exit 143/Garden Of The Gods Rd., then turn westbound onto Garden Of The Gods Rd., followed by a right onto N Cheyenne Cañon Rd. which will bring you straight into the Park.

GPS Coordinates: 38.7909865° N, 104.8653081° W

Best Time to Visit: Try visiting during the spring or fall for optimal weather conditions and fewer crowds!

Pass/Permit/Fees: All entrance fees at North Cheyenne Canon Park are free of charge, however, certain activities like camping may require a permit or special pass (see website for more information).

Did you Know? North Cheyenne Cañon Park is home to a variety of wildlife species, so keep an eye out for deer, elk, and other animals during your visit!

Website:https://coloradosprings.gov/NCC?fbclid=IwAR0tJQmjHnLA wPpicsNyyjtdb9yu3Y6ToU9qBUt7hyvefkz926OpAVI3yg

Colorado Springs Pioneers Museum

Take a journey through Colorado history at the Colorado Springs Pioneers Museum. Located in the central business district of the city, this museum offers visitors an immersive exploration of local culture and heritage. From artwork to artifacts, you can experience everything from early Native American life to present-day developments. Along with its permanent exhibits, the museum also showcases special collections that feature diverse topics like women's history and military veterans. Discover how Colorado has grown over its more than 150 years as a state!

Location: 215 S Tejon St, Colorado Springs, CO 80903-2206

Closest City or Town: Colorado Springs, Colorado

How to Get There: From downtown take E Platte Ave east until you reach S Tejon St., then turn right onto S Tejon Street for one block until you see the museum on your left side.

GPS Coordinates: 38.8303086° N, 104.8227987° W

Best Time to Visit: The Museum is open year-round with the exception of major holidays; spring and autumn months provide milder temperatures for outdoor activities in nearby parks such as Memorial Park or America The Beautiful Park while winter may be best enjoyed indoors exploring all this museum has to offer.

Pass/Permit/Fees: Admission is free but donations are accepted

Did you Know? The Colorado Springs Pioneers Museum offers educational programs for students of all ages in addition to their many exhibits and collections.

Website: http://www.cspm.org/

U.S. Olympic & Paralympic Museum

Experience history in the making at the US Olympic and Paralympic Museum in Colorado Springs, CO. This museum is dedicated to celebrating American athletes from both the Olympic and Paralympic Games, with interactive exhibits and artifacts that bring the spirit of sportsmanship alive. You'll learn about iconic Olympians like Jesse Owens and Wilma Rudolph while exploring exhibitions featuring sports such as track, swimming, basketball, gymnastics, and more! Whether you're a novice or an expert on the games, this museum has something for everyone!

Location: 200 S Sierra Madre St, Colorado Springs, CO 80903-3316

Closest City or Town: Colorado Springs, Colorado

How to Get There: From downtown take East Boulder Street south until you reach Sierra Madre St., then turn right onto S Sierra Madre and follow it for two blocks until you see the museum on your left side.

GPS Coordinates: 38.8294502° N, 104.8296896° W

Best Time to Visit: The Museum is open year-round with the exception of major holidays; spring and autumn months are ideal for visiting as temperatures tend to be milder during that season

Pass/Permit/Fees: Admission is $10-$15 depending on age

Did you Know? This museum houses more than 100 artifacts from past Olympic Games, some of which have never been seen before!

Website: http://usopm.org/

Will Rogers Memorial Shrine of the Sun

Step back in time at the Will Rogers Memorial Shrine of the Sun in Colorado Springs, CO. Originally built in 1935 as a tribute to the iconic actor, writer, and humorist, this picturesque memorial features lush landscaping and classic architecture that evoke an old-world charm. You can explore the magnificent Rose Garden with its meandering paths and tranquil ponds, or take in stunning views from atop Lookout Mountain. Whether you're a fan of Will Rogers or just want to get away for a peaceful stroll, this historic site is sure to enchant you!

Location: 4250 Cheyenne Mountain Zoo Rd, Colorado Springs, CO 80906-5728

Closest City or Town: Colorado Springs, Colorado

How to Get There: From downtown take South Nevada Ave south until you reach Cheyenne Mountain Zoo Rd., then follow it for two miles until you see the memorial on your left side.

GPS Coordinates: 38.7703821° N, 104.8550161° W

Best Time to Visit: The Memorial is open year-round with the exception of major holidays; spring and autumn months provide milder temperatures for outdoor activities in nearby parks such as Garden of Gods Park while winter can be enjoyed indoors exploring all this museum has to offer.

Pass/Permit/Fees: No entrance fees

Did you Know? This site is listed on the National Register of Historic Places!

Website: http://www.cmzoo.org/index.php/about-the-zoo/history/will-rogers-shrine/

Academy Riding Stables

Explore the incredible landscape of Colorado Springs on horseback with Academy Riding Stables! Tours run for two hours and take you through the lush meadows and breathtaking views of the Front Range. No experience is required but helmets are provided as a safety precaution. After your ride, you can explore the nearby historic ponds and waterfalls, or just take some time to relax in nature's serenity.

Location: 4 El Paso Blvd, Colorado Springs, CO 80904

Closest City or Town: Colorado Springs (located within city limits)

How to Get There: From downtown Colorado Springs take S 8th St until you reach El Paso Blvd. Turn left onto El Paso Blvd and follow it until you reach Academy Riding Stables.

GPS Coordinates: 38.8601691° N, 104.8868696° W

Best Time to Visit: Spring and autumn months are best as temperatures tend to be milder during this time.

Pass/Permit/Fees: Guided tours cost $70 per person for two hours or $115 for four hours. Please refer to their website for more information.

Did you Know? The stables have been offering guided horseback rides since the 1930s!

Website: http://www.academyridingstables.com/

CORTEZ

Hovenweep National Monument

Take a step back in time and explore the ancient ruins of Hovenweep National Monument, located in the Four Corners region of Cortez, Colorado. Rich with Native American history, this national monument features an array of archaeological sites dating back centuries. Take an interpretive tour or hike around to see the mysterious stone towers left behind by Pueblo people, listen to stories about their lives and customs, and marvel at the breathtaking views from atop Cajon Mesa.

Location: County Road 268A, Cortez, CO 84534

Closest City or Town: Cortez, Colorado (located within the city)

How to Get There: Take County Road N 2600 from Cortez and follow the signs for Hovenweep National Monument.

GPS Coordinates: 37.3488827° N, 108.5859265° W

Best Time to Visit: The park is open year-round but winter months have more desirable weather conditions for visiting outdoor attractions.

Pass/Permit/Fees: There's no entrance fee; however, there are fees for camping ($20) and guided tours ($10).

Did you Know? Hovenweep is one of four units that comprise Canyons Of The Ancients National Monument – making it part of a larger area rich in archeological sites!

Website: https://www.nps.gov/hove

CRESTED BUTTE

Kebler Pass

Experience some of Colorado's best autumn colors at Kebler Pass, a scenic drive through Gunnison National Forest. Follow the 25-mile loop that takes you up to 9,000 feet across meadows and mountains for breathtaking panoramic views of aspens and evergreens. This byway passes through several small towns such as Paonia and Crested Butte offering plenty of opportunity for stops along the way.

Location: Colorado 81230, United States

Closest City or Town: Crested Butte, Colorado (just a short drive away)

How to Get There: Take Hwy 133 from Crested Butte until you reach Kebler Pass Rd., then take a turn onto County Road 12 heading west.

GPS Coordinates: 38.5084518° N, 106.8178377° W

Best Time to Visit: Late August and early September are the best times of year for taking in the full beauty of Kebler Pass.

Pass/Permit/Fees: Entrance is free; however, there may be a fee for some summertime activities.

Did you Know? The Kebler Pass area is known as one of Colorado's most beautiful fall foliage displays!

Website: https://www.uncovercolorado.com/scenic-drives/kebler-pass/

CRIPPLE CREEK

Mollie Kathleen Gold Mine

Take a journey back into mining history at the Mollie Kathleen Gold Mine in Cripple Creek, Colorado. Named after the first woman in Colorado to strike gold, this mine offers visitors an exciting underground exploration of its mining tunnels. You can take a guided tour and learn about the history of gold mining while discovering stunning formations that have been untouched for over 100 years.

Location: 1 Mile N. Hwy 67, Cripple Creek, CO 80813

Closest City or Town: Cripple Creek, Colorado (located within the city)

How to Get There: Take Highway 67 north from downtown Cripple Creek until you reach the Mollie Kathleen Gold Mine entrance on your left.

GPS Coordinates: 38.7466555° N, 105.1783149° W

Best Time to Visit: The mine is open year-round but the best time of year for taking a tour is during summer months when temperatures are milder.

Pass/Permit/Fees: Entrance fees vary based on the type of tour chosen and number of participants, ranging from $19-$35 per person.

Did you Know? Mollie Kathleen Gold Mine is one of the most productive gold mines in Colorado, with more than 300,000 ounces extracted since it opened in 1892!

Website: http://www.goldminetours.com/

DENVER

Escapology

Take your adventure to new heights at Escapology, an interactive escape room experience located in Denver's historic LoDo neighborhood. With a range of rooms and puzzles designed for all levels of skill and bravery, you're sure to find the challenge that's perfect for you! Work together as a team or solve the puzzles solo - whichever way you choose, this is an unforgettable journey into another world!

Location: 2220 California St, Denver, CO 80205-2824

Closest City or Town: Denver, Colorado (located within the city)

How to Get There: From downtown Denver take 15th Street eastbound until you reach Wazee Street. Turn left onto Market Street then right on 20th street before turning left onto California Street where Escapology can be found.

GPS Coordinates: 39.7509083° N, 104.9842711° W

Best Time to Visit: Open year-round; however peak times are Friday and Saturday nights when reservations often book up quickly so it's best to plan ahead!

Pass/Permit/Fees: Prices vary depending on group size ($27-$37 per person). Please visit their website for more details.

Did you Know? Escapology offers a range of custom-themed rooms to choose from such as "The Study" and "Da Vinci's Challenge" for even more fun and excitement!

Website: http://www.escapology.com/denver

Denver Mountain Parks

Discover one of Denver's hidden gems - the stunning network of mountain parks owned and managed by the city. Over 14,000 acres in size, these picturesque recreational areas offer everything from hiking, running, biking, camping, fishing, and bird-watching opportunities to disc golf courses and picnic spots with breathtaking views. Located in Clear Creek Canyon near Golden Colorado, this is the perfect place to explore nature without leaving the city limits!

Location: 3000 E 1st Ave, Denver, CO 80206-5638

Closest City or Town: Golden, Colorado (just a short drive away)

How to Get There: From downtown Denver take I-70 W until you reach US 40 W/6th Ave. Turn right onto 19th Street then left on Golden Gate Canyon Rd., and follow it into Clear Creek Canyon where you will find signs for the park entrances.

GPS Coordinates: 39.7168183° N, 104.9526302° W

Best Time to Visit: May through October when the weather is milder and most of the trails are open for exploration

Pass/Permit/Fees: Entrance is free; however, there may be fees for some activities such as camping and fishing. Please visit their website for more details.

Did you Know? Denver Mountain Parks is home to over 30 miles of trails including the historic Apex Trail, which dates back to 1913!

Website: http://denvermountainparks.org/

Denver Botanic Gardens

Experience an unexpected oasis in the heart of the city at the Denver Botanic Gardens. Here you can wander through acres of lush gardens filled with exotic flora from around the world, explore a serene Japanese garden, take a guided tour through one of North America's largest collections of orchids, or simply find a shady spot and watch butterflies flit by. Whatever you do, the gardens offer a welcome respite from the hustle and bustle of city life!

Location: 1007 York Street, Denver, CO 80206-3014

Closest City or Town: Denver, Colorado (located within the city)

How to Get There: From downtown Denver take I-25 N until you reach Speer Blvd. Turn left onto 9th Avenue before turning right on York Street where the gardens can be found.

GPS Coordinates: 39.7319003° N, 104.9629115° W

Best Time to Visit: April through October when conditions are milder and there is an abundance of blooms in all directions!

Pass/Permit/Fees: There is an admission fee to enter the gardens (children 12 and under are free). Please visit their website for more details.

Did you Know? Denver Botanic Gardens won the prestigious U.S. 2006 Green Globe Award for its commitment to environmental sustainability!

Website: http://www.botanicgardens.org/

Coors Field

Explore the home of the Colorado Rockies at Coors Field in Denver. Catch a game and enjoy classic ballpark favorites like hot dogs, nachos, peanuts, popcorn, and cold beer. Or take an interactive tour to learn about the stadium's history and behind-the-scenes access to some of its best features.

Location: 2001 Blake St At 20th St, Denver, CO 80205-2060

Closest City or Town: Denver, Colorado (located within the city)

How to Get There: By car from downtown Denver travel northwest on 20th St until you reach Blake St., and turn left onto it until you see signs for Coors Field.

GPS Coordinates: 39.7556863° N, 104.9941774° W

Best Time to Visit: The baseball season runs March through October; however Peak fall foliage is also spectacular in September/October!

Pass/Permit/Fees: Ticket prices vary depending on the game; please check their website for more details.

Did you Know? Baseball fans are sure to recognize this iconic destination—it was featured as part of the movie "The Big Lebowski"!

Website: https://www.mlb.com/rockies/ballpark

Denver Museum of Nature & Science

Discover the wonders of the natural world at the Denver Museum of Nature & Science. From permanent and changing exhibits to educational programs and special events, the museum offers a wide range of activities to engage and inspire visitors of all ages. Explore dinosaur fossils, learn about the history of Colorado and the universe in the Gates Planetarium, or take a trip through time in the Prehistoric Journey exhibit.

Location: 2001 N Colorado Blvd, Denver, CO 80205-5798

Closest City or Town: Denver, Colorado (located within the city)

How to Get There: By car from downtown Denver take Colfax Ave west until you reach Colorado Blvd; turn left onto it and follow signs leading to the Museum.

GPS Coordinates: 39.7472834° N, 104.9430834° W

Best Time to Visit: Summer months are ideal as temperatures tend to be milder and more conducive to exploring the outdoors.

Pass/Permit/Fees: Admission fees vary depending on activities ($5-$30). Please visit their website for more details.

Did you Know? The Museum of Nature & Science was founded in 1900 by the Denver Women's Club, making it one of the oldest museums in Colorado!

Website: http://www.dmns.org/

Mount Evans

Climb to an elevation of 14,264 feet and experience breathtaking alpine views at Mount Evans in Colorado. Take a scenic drive along America's Highest Byway or explore miles of hiking trails that wind through forests and meadows—all leading up to the summit of the mountain. Spot wildflowers, marmots, and colorful birds along the way, or camp under the starry desert sky for a truly memorable experience.

Location: Mount Evans Parking, 16 Mount Evans Hwy, Idaho Springs, CO 80452

Closest City or Town: Idaho Springs, Colorado (located nearby)

How to Get There: By car from Denver take I-70 West towards Idaho Springs; Exit 240 will lead you directly onto Mt. Evans Road until you reach the parking area.

GPS Coordinates: 39.5877393° N, 105.6423372° W

Best Time to Visit: Summer months are ideal as temperatures tend to be milder and more conducive to exploring the outdoors.

Pass/Permit/Fees: Entrance fees are required for vehicles ($10). Please visit their website for more details.

Did you Know? Mount Evans is the highest peak in the Front Range of Colorado and was named after John C. Evans, a former Governor of Colorado!

Website: https://www.colorado.com/scenic-historic-byway/mount-evans-scenic-and-historic-byway

Molly Brown House Museum

Located in the heart of Denver, Colorado, the Molly Brown House Museum offers a unique glimpse into Denver's past. Step inside the beautiful 1899 Queen Anne-style mansion to explore its classic Victorian architecture and learn about the life of Titanic survivor Margaret "Molly" Brown. Stroll through eight rooms filled with original artifacts and period furnishings for an immersive experience that brings history to life.

Location: 1340 N Pennsylvania St, Denver, CO 80203-2417

Closest City or Town: Denver, Colorado

How to Get There: Take Colfax Avenue East until you reach Pennsylvania Street; turn right onto Pennsylvania Street and continue for one mile until you reach the museum on your left.

GPS Coordinates: 39.7374933° N, 104.9807338° W

Best Time to Visit: Spring and Summer months are the best time for visiting as days tend to be longer during that season

Pass/Permit/Fees: Admission fees vary depending on age ($8-$12). Please visit their website for more details.

Did you Know? Molly Brown was an outspoken socialite who championed causes such as women's suffrage and workers' rights.

Website: http://www.mollybrown.org/

Empower Field at Mile High

Experience the thrill of a live football game at Empower Field at Mile High, home to the Denver Broncos! Feel the energy of 76,125 cheering fans as you watch your favorite team take on their rivals in this state-of-the-art stadium. Take a break from the action to explore level five for interactive games, grab some grub at one of the many concession stands, or visit Sports Legends Mall to find exclusive merchandise and memorabilia. With plenty to do and see, Empower Field is an unforgettable experience!

Location: 1701 Bryant St, Denver, CO 80204-1701

Closest City or Town: Denver, Colorado

How to Get There: Take Colfax Avenue West until you reach Federal Boulevard; turn left onto Federal Boulevard and continue for two miles until you reach the stadium on your right.

GPS Coordinates: 39.7441196° N, 105.0203951° W

Best Time to Visit: Fall months are the best time for visiting as that's when football season is in full swing.

Pass/Permit/Fees: Ticket prices vary depending on the game schedule ($20-$200). Please visit their website for more details.

Did you Know? In 2018, Empower Field at Mile High was ranked number two out of all 32 NFL stadiums by USA Today.

Website: http://www.sportsauthorityfieldatmilehigh.com/

Stranahan's Whiskey Distillery & Cocktail Bar

Head to Stranahan's Whiskey Distillery & Cocktail Bar for a truly unique experience! Take one of their signature tours and learn about the processes they use to make their award-winning whiskey, sample straight from the barrel, and sip on specialty cocktails made with house-made syrups and bitters. End your visit at the rooftop bar to soak in sweeping views of Denver while sipping on a refreshing drink!

Location: 200 S Kalamath St, Denver, CO 80223-1813

Closest City or Town: Denver, Colorado

How to Get There: Take I-25 South until you reach 6th Avenue; take the exit and turn right onto Kalamath Street and continue for one mile until you reach the distillery on your left.

GPS Coordinates: 39.712484° N, 104.9986722° W

Best Time to Visit: Spring through Fall months are the best time for visiting as days tend to be longer during that season

Pass/Permit/Fees: Tour prices vary depending on type ($15-$95). Please visit their website for more details.

Did you Know? Stranahan's has won numerous awards including Double Gold at San Francisco World Spirits Competition in 2018.

Website: http://www.stranahans.com/tours/

Mount Evans Scenic Byway

Take a drive through the sky on the highest paved road in North America, Mount Evans Scenic Byway. Located near Idaho Springs, Colorado, this 28-mile stretch of highway takes you up to 14,258 feet above sea level to enjoy stunning panoramic views of mountains and forests. Along the way, you can marvel at ancient glaciers and tundra vegetation unique to high altitudes. Don't forget your camera – wildlife sightings such as mountain goats are common!

Location: PFQG+FX Idaho Springs, Colorado, United States

Closest City or Town: Idaho Springs

How to Get There: From Idaho Springs, take US-40 W then merge onto I-70 E. Take exit 240 for Mount Evans Road and head north to reach the scenic byway.

GPS Coordinates: 39.7386875° N, 105.5225625° W

Best Time to Visit: Summer months are best during daylight hours since snow may block some parts of the road during wintertime

Pass/Permit/Fees: Entrance fees vary depending on activities ($5-$30)

Did you Know? The summit has been nicknamed "The Top Of The Rockies" due to its magnificent surroundings

Website: http://www.codot.gov/travel/scenic-byways/north-central/mount-evans

The International Church of Cannabis

Welcome to 'Elevationism' - a religion that celebrates and promotes the spiritual benefits of cannabis! The International Church of Cannabis is located in Denver, Colorado, and follows a belief system focused on the exploration of inner peace and happiness. Whether you're there to take part in one of their weekly services or just to admire the spectacular murals adorning the walls, this church is sure to add some color to your life.

Location: 400 S Logan St, Denver, CO 80209-1817

Closest City or Town: Denver

How to Get There: From downtown Denver take 10th Ave/US-87 N until you reach E Bayaud Ave. Turn right onto S Logan St., then follow it until you see the church on your left.

GPS Coordinates: 39.7091597° N, 104.9822776° W

Best Time to Visit: Year-round

Pass/Permit/Fees: Entrance is free of charge

Did you Know? Children are allowed to visit the church as long as they're accompanied by an adult!

Website: http://www.elevationists.org/

Washington Park

Take a stroll around one of Denver's most iconic parks, Washington Park - home to two lakes, multiple trails, and lush gardens. Listen to the wind rustle through the trees and discover hidden gems like 'The Spirit of Colorado' sculpture from artist John Henne. With its numerous attractions, this urban oasis makes a great spot for a quick escape from the city.

Location: S. Downing St. & E. Louisiana Ave, Denver, CO 80209

Closest City or Town: Denver

How to Get There: Take I-25 N until you reach exit 209A for Colorado Blvd/US-287 E. Merge onto S Downing St and turn right onto E Louisiana Ave to enter the park.

GPS Coordinates: 39.6929737° N, 104.9734274° W

Best Time to Visit: Year-round

Pass/Permit/Fees: Entrance is free of charge

Did you Know? Washington Park features over 155 species of trees!

Website: https://www.denver.org/listing/washington-park/6828/

Forney Museum of Transportation

Located in Denver, Colorado, the Forney Museum of Transportation is the perfect place to explore and discover the history and evolution of vehicles. From vintage cars and locomotives to airplanes, wagons, electric vehicles, bicycles, and much more - this museum has something for everyone! Explore interactive exhibits that will transport you back in time with artifacts detailing every era from 1830 onwards. It's a fascinating journey through history that kids are sure to love!

Location: 4303 Brighton Blvd, Denver, CO 80216-3702

Closest City or Town: Denver, Colorado (located within city limits)

How to Get There: Take I-25 Northbound towards Downtown Denver until you reach exit 212A on your right for Park Avenue West. Turn left onto Park Ave W then turn right onto Brighton Blvd - follow signs for Forney Museum until you find the parking lot at 4303 Brighton Blvd.

GPS Coordinates: 39.6929737° N, 104.9734274° W

Best Time to Visit: Open year-round but mild temperatures make it most pleasant during the fall months

Pass/Permit/Fees: Admission is $10 for adults; free admission for children under 12 years old

Did you Know? The museum was founded by J.D. Forney, a former Denver city auditor who was passionate about preserving the history of transportation!

Website: http://www.forneymuseum.org/

The Denver Center for the Performing Arts

It's time to experience something truly extraordinary at The Denver Center for the Performing Arts! Located in downtown Denver, this is a world-class performing arts center with three theater complexes offering an array of live performances. From classical operas to blockbuster musicals, you can enjoy some of the best theatrical productions right here! It's also home to events like film festivals and conferences - come explore this vibrant cultural hub and feel inspired!

Location: 1101 13th St Theatres are located at 14th & Curtis streets, Denver, CO 80204-5319

Closest City or Town: Denver, Colorado (located within city limits)

How to Get There: Take I-25 Northbound until you get to exit 210A on your right for 14th St. Turn left onto 14th St, then turn right onto Curtis St, and follow signs for Denver Center for the Performing Arts until you find the parking lot at 1101 13th Street.

GPS Coordinates: 39.7453453° N, 104.997198° W

Best Time to Visit: Open year round but most enjoyable during mild fall months

Pass/Permit/Fees: Varies depending on the show or event; please check their website for more information.

Did you Know? The Denver Center was founded in 1972 and has been a thriving center of culture and entertainment ever since!

Website: http://www.denvercenter.org/

Denver Public Library

Explore the pages of history at the Denver Public Library - it's one of the most iconic institutions in the city! Located right downtown, this library features five floors of books, periodicals, multimedia collections, and other resources for researchers and students alike. Take a break from the bustling city streets and relax in its inviting atmosphere; for many people, it's their favorite spot to hang out on any given day.

Location: 10 West 14th Parkway, Denver, CO 80204

Closest City or Town: Denver, Colorado (located within city limits)

How to Get There: Take I-25 Southbound until you get to exit 212A on your right for Park Avenue West. Turn left onto Park Ave W, then take the first right onto 14th St and follow signs for Denver Public Library until you find the parking lot at 10 West 14th Parkway.

GPS Coordinates: 39.737308° N, 104.988128° W

Best Time to Visit: Open year-round but mild temperatures make it most pleasant during the fall months

Pass/Permit/Fees: Free admission

Did you Know? The library holds over two million books, making it one of the largest collections in the state!

Website: http://www.denverlibrary.org/

Cathedral of the Immaculate Conception

Step into this stunning 19th-century cathedral, located in Denver's Capitol Hill neighborhood. Built from 1888 to 1912 and modeled after the European Gothic style of architecture, it features soaring ceilings, elaborate stained glass windows, a 40-foot bell tower, and beautiful works of art. Explore its many hidden gems on a guided tour or experience its grandeur during one of its daily services. **Location:** 1530 N Logan St., Denver CO 80203

Closest City or Town: Denver

How to Get There: Located in downtown Denver near Civic Center Park, visitors can take the 16th Street Mall Free Shuttle for easy access.

GPS Coordinates: 39.740737° N, 104.981971° W

Best Time to Visit: Open year-round – Summer months are the best time for visiting as the weather tends to be milder

Pass/Permit/Fees: Entrance is free

Did you Know? The Cathedral was built by Italian stonemasons who had immigrated from Tuscany that same year

Website: http://www.denvercathedral.org/

Clyfford Still Museum

Explore modernist artwork at this unique museum dedicated to abstract expressionism pioneer Clyfford Still. Located in Denver's Golden Triangle Creative District, the museum houses a vast collection of artworks created by the influential 20th-century artist, including his signature paintings and rarely-seen works from the 1940s to 1960s. Visitors can also take in the beautiful architecture of this former industrial building as they explore its galleries and public spaces.

Location: 1250 Bannock St., Denver CO 80204-3631

Closest City or Town: Denver

How to Get There: Take 13th Avenue south towards Broadway until you reach Acoma Street. Turn left onto Bannock Street and follow it

1 block until you see signs for Clyfford Still Museum on your right-hand side.

GPS Coordinates: 39.7362374° N, 104.98968° W

Best Time to Visit: Open year-round – Summer months are the best time for visiting as the weather tends to be milder

Pass/Permit/Fees: Entrance fees vary depending on activities ($6-$10). Please visit their website for more details.

Did you Know? The museum is housed in the former National Wax Museum building, which was built in 1917 but has undergone extensive renovations?

Website: http://clyffordstillmuseum.org/

Kirkland Museum of Fine & Decorative Art

Experience fine art and decorative works from around the world at Kirkland Museum of Fine & Decorative Art. Located in Denver's Golden Triangle Creative District, the museum houses a unique collection of art from the late 19th century to the present day. Visitors can explore works ranging from ceramic pottery and glasswork to vintage posters and quilts spread across three floors of gallery spaces.

Location: 1201 Bannock Street, Denver CO 80204

Closest City or Town: Denver

How to Get There: Take 13th Avenue south towards Broadway until you reach Acoma Street. Turn left onto Bannock Street and follow it 2 blocks until you see signs for Kirkland Museum on your right-hand side.

GPS Coordinates: 39.7356446° N, 104.9905928° W

Best Time to Visit: Open year-round – Summer months are the best time for visiting as the weather tends to be milder

Pass/Permit/Fees: The entrance fee is $10. Please visit their website for more details.

Did you Know? The museum's building was once a former garage and auto shop?

Website: http://www.kirklandmuseum.org/

Dillon Reservoir

Discover the hidden beauty of Dillon Reservoir, a stunning lake located in the heart of Colorado. Surrounded by mountain peaks and pine-filled forests, this is the perfect spot for an outdoor adventure. Enjoy boating, fishing, camping, and hiking along its shores, or take part in snow sports like ice skating and snowmobiling when temperatures drop. For breathtaking views that will last you a lifetime, look no further than Dillon Reservoir!

Location: 203 W Lodgepole St., Dillon CO 80435

Closest City or Town: Dillon Colorado (located within city limits)

How to Get There: Head southwest on I-70 E and then take exit 205 until you reach US 6. Turn right onto US 6/Loveland Pass Rd., continue until you see W Lodgepole St., turn left to get to Dakota Reservoir's parking area.

GPS Coordinates: 39.6253329° N, 106.0465904° W

Best Time to Visit: Summer months are ideal for enjoying watersports while winter offers fun activities such as ice skating at frozen lakeshores.

Pass/Permit/Fees: No entrance fee but visitors must purchase a Colorado state fishing license if they plan to fish.

Did you Know? The Dillon Reservoir is the largest body of water in Summit County, and it is supplied by the Blue River.

Website:
http://www.dillonrangerdistrict.com/summer/olddilres_hkg.htm

DINOSAUR

Dinosaur National Monument

Embark on a journey into the past at Dinosaur National Monument, a rugged terrain that preserves one of the world's most famous fossil beds. Located in Northwestern Colorado near the Utah border, this monument offers dramatic mountain desert landscapes with incredible opportunities for adventure and exploration. Whether you're looking for scenic hikes or ancient relics of our prehistoric ancestors, this is an essential stop on any traveler's itinerary!

Location: 4545 Highway 40 Quarry Visitor Center, Dinosaur, CO 81610-9724

Closest City or Town: Vernal, Utah (45 miles away)

How to Get There: From Vernal take US-191 S until you reach Highway 40 E/UT-64 E (near Jensen). Take UT-64 E/Highway 40 E until you reach Quarry Visitor Center in Dinosaur, CO

GPS Coordinates: 40.2430227° N, 108.9738105° W

Best Time to Visit: The best time for visiting is during autumn when temperatures are milder **Pass/Permit/Fees:** Entrance fees vary depending on activities ($5-$30)

Did you Know? This national monument was named after more than 1,500 dinosaur fossils discovered here!

Website: https://www.nps.gov/dino

DIVIDE

Colorado Wolf and Wildlife Center

Discover a unique wildlife experience at the Colorado Wolf and Wildlife Center! Located near Divide, CO this sanctuary offers educational tours about wolves, foxes, coyotes, and more. Listen to stories from passionate staff members as you learn about wolf behavior, biology, and conservation efforts on these animals' behalf. Participate in an interactive feeding tour and take breathtaking photos of the wildlife around you.

Location: Lower Twin Rocks Road, Divide, CO 80814

Closest City or Town: Divide Colorado (located within city limits)

How to Get There: Head south from I-25 S and then take exit 131 until you reach US-24 W. Turn right onto Lower Twin Rocks Rd., until you see the signage for the Center's entrance.

GPS Coordinates: 38.92348° N, 105.2279439° W

Best Time to Visit: Summer months are ideal for experiencing the tours given by knowledgeable staff members

Pass/Permit/Fees: Entrance fees vary depending on the activity chosen ($20-$50). Please visit their website for more details.

Did you Know? The Colorado Wolf and Wildlife Center is a non-profit organization that has been dedicated to the care of wolf hybrids since 1993.

Website: http://www.wolfeducation.org/

DURANGO

Snowmobile Adventures

Experience an unforgettable adventure at Snowmobile Adventures! Located in Durango, CO, this facility offers guided snowmobiling tours through some of the most beautiful landscapes in the area. Get ready to explore frozen lakes, open meadows, and rocky trails while enjoying breathtaking views from atop your snowmobile. During winter months, you can even experience night rides under dazzling stars!

Location: 1 Skier Pl., Durango, CO 81301

Closest City or Town: Durango Colorado (located within city limits)

How to Get There: Head north from US-550 and then take I-70 W until you reach Exit 263/Durango. Turn onto Camino Del Rio S., and follow it until you see Skier Pl., turn right to get to Snowmobile Adventures' parking area.

GPS Coordinates: 37.6308747° N, 107.8142853° W

Best Time to Visit: Winter months are ideal for experiencing the snowmobiling tours offered by Snowmobile Adventures.

Pass/Permit/Fees: Entrance fees range between $279-$349 depending on the type of tour chosen.

Did you Know? Snowmobile Adventures offers custom tours tailored to fit your individual needs.

Website: http://www.snowmobiledurango.com/

Durango and Silverton Narrow Gauge Railroad and Museum

Step into the Wild West with a visit to Durango and Silverton Narrow Gauge Railroad, an iconic 19th-century steam engine train that takes you on an unforgettable journey through Colorado's breathtaking mountain landscape. Marvel at ancient canyons, cascading waterfalls, lush forests, and wildflower fields during your 3-hour round-trip ride. You can also explore the museum to learn more about the area's unique history.

Location: 479 Main St., Durango, CO 81301-5421

Closest City or Town: Durango, Colorado (located within the city)

How to Get There: Located in downtown Durango right by Main Avenue Station—the departure station for Boarding Train Ride excursions—the railroad is easily accessible from all directions of downtown via public transportation or private vehicle.

GPS Coordinates: 37.3297286° N, 107.7999902° W

Best Time to Visit: Peak season runs from late April until mid-October when visitors have access to daily excursions as well as special events such as Murder Mystery Dinners aboard The Animas Canyon Railway Dinner Train!

Pass/Permit/Fees: Ticket prices vary depending on the type of excursion chosen. Please visit the website for more details.

Did you Know? The Durango and Silverton Narrow Gauge Railroad is part of Colorado's rich history, having been in operation since 1882!

Website: http://www.durangotrain.com/

Historic Downtown Durango

Immerse yourself in the vibrant culture and heritage of Historic Downtown Durango, a charming district that brings together local businesses, galleries, eateries, and a variety of special events taking place year-round. Explore the area's unique architecture as you stroll along Main Avenue shopping for souvenirs or grab a bite at one of the many restaurants.

Location: 850 1/2 Main Ave Suite 2, Durango, CO 81301-5434

Closest City or Town: Durango, Colorado (located within the city)

How to Get There: Located in downtown Durango right off Main Avenue—the main thoroughfare of the Historic Downtown District—the area is easily accessible from all directions via public transportation or private vehicle.

GPS Coordinates: 37.2729557° N, 107.880741° W

Best Time to Visit: The best time to visit Historic Downtown would be during the summer months when many special events take place such as Cinco de Mayo celebrations, the Durango Farmers Market, and more.

Pass/Permit/Fees: Most events in Historic Downtown are free and open to all. Please check the website for exact fees when applicable.

Did you Know? The historic Strater Hotel is an iconic destination in downtown Durango—it opened its doors back in 1887!

Website: http://www.downtowndurango.org/

San Juan National Forest

Escape to San Juan National Forest, a captivating mountain range that takes you on a journey of lush forests, jagged peaks, wildflower meadows, and diverse wildlife. Explore the area's various trails on foot or bike, go fishing in the nearby rivers and lakes, or take part in guided wilderness tours.

Location: 15 Burnett Ct, Durango, CO 81301-3647

Closest City or Town: Durango, Colorado

How to Get There: San Juan National Forest is located about 10 miles south of downtown Durango. Accessible by road from Highway 550 South via US 160 E/CO 172 W.

GPS Coordinates: 37.2732478° N, 107.893284° W

Best Time to Visit: The best time to visit San Juan National Forest would be during the summer months when days are long and sunny with pleasant temperatures perfect for outdoor activities.

Pass/Permit/Fees: There is no entrance fee to access the national forest, however, visitors should check for fire restrictions and camping fees before planning their trip.

Did you Know? San Juan National Forest is home to a variety of amazing wildlife which include elk, black bears, bighorn sheep, mule deer, and more!

Website: http://www.fs.fed.us/r2/sanjuan/

Animas River Trail

Explore the stunning beauty of Colorado on the Animas River Trail. Located in Durango, this loop trail offers hikers and bikers a chance to experience majestic views, take in local wildlife, and even spot some petroglyphs left behind by ancient Native American cultures. A perfect way to explore nature while staying close to town!

Location: 802 Main Avenue | Durango, CO 81301

Closest City or Town: Durango, Colorado

How to Get There: Take US-160 W until you reach Main Avenue/CO-3 S. Turn right onto Main Avenue for 0.6 miles before turning left onto East 2nd Ave., where you will see signs for the Animas River Trailhead parking lot shortly after turning onto E 2nd Ave...

GPS Coordinates: 37.2724227° N, 107.880764° W

Best Time to Visit: Spring is an ideal time for visiting as wildflowers are blooming and temperatures are milder than summer months when afternoon thunderstorms can occur frequently due to seasonal monsoons moving through the area.

Pass/Permit/Fees: None required but entrance fees may apply at certain sites within the trail.

Did you Know? The Animas River Trail is part of the Colorado Trail, a 500-mile hiking path that stretches from Denver to Durango!

Website: https://www.durango.org/plan/maps/animas-river-trail-map/

Animas River

Soak up some sun while floating down the Animas River in Durango, Colorado! This popular spot for tubing and rafting winds through stunning canyons lined with vibrant blooms during the spring months. Take a leisurely ride or go for an adrenaline rush on the rapids, either way, it's sure to be an unforgettable experience!

Location: Schneider Park, Durango, CO 81301

Closest City or Town: Durango, Colorado

How to Get There: Take US-550 S and turn left onto US-160 W. Turn right onto Goeglein Gulch Rd., then left onto CR 203/Herman Gulch Rd.

Follow it until you reach Schneider Park Rd., where the Animas River access point is located.

GPS Coordinates: 37.2781864° N, 107.882483° W

Best Time to Visit: Summer months are best for visiting as temperatures are milder during this season with daily rains that help keep the river cool.

Pass/Permit/Fees: None required but entrance fees may apply at certain sites within the river access area.

Did you Know? The Animas River was once an important supply route for the Ute and Navajo tribes who called this area home!

Website: http://vacationdurango.com/animas-river-trail

ESTES PARK

Rocky Mountains

Discover a world of adventure in Colorado's Rocky Mountains! From majestic hiking trails to crystal-clear mountain lakes, there is plenty to explore here. Take some time to fish or spot local wildlife along the way, and don't forget your camera for those stunning views!

Location: 88V8+4G Estes Park, Colorado

Closest City or Town: Estes Park, Colorado

How to Get There: Take US-36 W to Estes Park. Turn right onto MacGregor Ave. and continue until you reach the Rocky Mountains National Park entrance.

GPS Coordinates: 40.3428125° N, 105.6836875° W

Best Time to Visit: The best time to visit is from late spring to early fall when snowstorms are less likely and temperatures are milder for outdoor activities and sightseeing.

Pass/Permit/Fees: A park pass is required for entry into Rocky Mountain National Park which can be purchased online or at the entrance station upon arriving at the park.

Did you Know? Rocky Mountain National Park is home to over 60 species of mammals and more than 280 species of birds!

Website: http://rockymountainnationalpark.com/

National Park Gateway Stables

Explore the spectacular Rocky Mountain National Park on horseback! Located just a short drive from the picturesque town of Estes Park, Colorado, this family-run stable offers guided rides in the area's breathtaking landscapes. Choose your favorite horse from their gentle and well-trained herd and meander along trails overlooking pristine alpine lakes, evergreen forests, and snowcapped peaks. Whether you're an experienced rider or a beginner looking to experience the wilds for the first time, there's something here for everyone—no matter what adventure you seek.

Location: 4600 Fall River Road, Estes Park CO 80517-9219

Closest City or Town: Estes Park (located within city limits)

How to Get There: From downtown Estes Park take US Hwy 34 East until you reach Fall River Rd., turn left onto Fall River Rd., then follow it until you see signs for The Gateway Stables entrance.

GPS Coordinates: 40.4020907° N, 105.586822° W

Best Time to Visit: The best time of year to visit is during summer through fall when temperatures are milder and visitors can enjoy outdoor activities without the extreme cold.

Pass/Permit/Fees: Prices range for different packages and experiences, please visit their website to learn more about pricing options.

Did you Know? National Park Gateway Stables is a family-owned business, established in 1905!

Website: http://www.skhorses.com/

Cowpoke Corner Corral

For an unforgettable outdoor experience, explore Rocky Mountain National Park in style on horseback from Cowpoke Corner Corral! This stable offers guided rides on gentle horses sure-footed enough to traverse rugged mountain terrain, allowing you to take in sweeping views of snow-capped peaks, lush meadows, and pristine alpine lakes. Whether you're looking for a leisurely stroll or an action-packed adventure, Cowpoke Corner Corral has the perfect horseback ride for you.

Location: 2166 State Highway 66, Estes Park CO 80517-8320

Closest City or Town: Estes Park (located within city limits)

How to Get There: From downtown Estes Park take US Hwy 34 East until you reach "Moraine Avenue" turn right onto Moraine Ave., then follow it until you see signs for the Cowpoke Corner Corral entrance.

GPS Coordinates: 40.3545583° N, 105.5604897° W

Best Time to Visit: The best time of year to visit is during summer through fall when temperatures are milder and visitors can enjoy outdoor activities without the extreme cold.

Pass/Permit/Fees: Prices range for different packages and experiences, please visit their website to learn more about pricing options.

Did you Know? The horses of Cowpoke Corner Corral have been featured in various Hollywood movies!

Website: http://www.skhorses.com/Cowpoke.html

Bear Lake

Discover the beauty of Colorado's Rocky Mountains at Bear Lake! Located in Estes Park, this stunning lake is surrounded by breathtaking scenery including snow-capped peaks, lush meadows, evergreen forests, and an array of wildflowers that bloom in summer months. Boating, fishing, and hiking are just some of the activities you can enjoy at this idyllic lake. Pack a picnic lunch and let yourself be immersed in nature's beauty!

Location: Estes Park CO 80517

Closest City or Town: Estes Park (located within city limits)

How to Get There: From downtown Estes Park take US Hwy 34 East until you reach Bear Lake Rd., turn right onto Bear Lake Rd., then follow it until you see signs for the entrance of the lake.

GPS Coordinates: 40.3772059° N, 105.5216651° W

Best Time to Visit: The best time of year to visit is during summer through fall when temperatures are milder and visitors can enjoy outdoor activities without the extreme cold.

Pass/Permit/Fees: Bear Lake is free to visit with no passes required.

Did you Know? The Bear Lake area was founded in 1820 by trappers!

Website: https://www.nps.gov/romo/index.htm

Emerald Lake Trail

Discover the beauty of nature on the Emerald Lake Trail, located in Estes Park, Colorado. Nestled within Rocky Mountain National Park, this scenic 1.8-mile loop trail is lined with lush green meadows and towering evergreen trees surrounding a stunning lake. Follow the trail to reach Alberta Falls or embark on a longer journey and explore the

Continental Divide Trail via Sprague Lake. With plenty of breathtaking views along the way, don't forget to bring your camera!

Location: 8936+FQ Estes Park, CO 80517

Closest City or Town: Estes Park, Colorado

How to Get There: Take US-34 W from downtown Estes Park towards Moraine Avenue for 4 miles until you reach Bear Lake Road. Turn left onto Bear Lake Rd and follow it until you see signs for the Emerald Lake parking area on your left side (0.5 mile).

GPS Coordinates: 40.3772059° N, 105.5216651° W

Best Time to Visit: Summer months are the best time for visiting as temperatures tend to be milder during that season

Pass/Permit/Fees: Entrance fees vary depending on the activities. Please visit their website for more details.

Did you Know? The Emerald Lake Trail is a popular destination and it can get crowded during peak seasons, so arrive early to beat the crowds.

Website: http://www.nps.gov/thingstodo/romo_emeraldlake.htm

Alberta Falls

Take a break from your journey to explore Alberta Falls, located in Estes Park, Colorado within Rocky Mountain National Park! This 30-foot waterfall cascades over large boulders and into a beautiful pool below, creating an enchanting atmosphere that can't be missed! Take pictures of the breathtaking scenery or embark on a hike along the Continental Divide Trail via Sprague Lake to reach even better views.

Location: 8936+FQ Estes Park, Colorado

Closest City or Town: Estes Park, Colorado

How to Get There: Take US-34 W from downtown Estes Park towards Moraine Avenue for 4 miles until you reach Bear Lake Road. Turn left onto Bear Lake Rd and follow it until you see signs for Alberta Falls on your right side (3.2 mile).

GPS Coordinates: 40.3036875° N, 105.6380625° W

Best Time to Visit: Summer months are the best time for visiting as temperatures tend to be milder during that season

Pass/Permit/Fees: Entrance fees vary depending on the activities. Please visit their website for more details.

Did you Know? Alberta Falls is one of the most popular destinations in Rocky Mountain National Park!

Website: http://www.nps.gov/romo/planyourvisit/hikes.htm

Sprague Lake

Take a break from your hike and enjoy the peaceful atmosphere of Sprague Lake, located in Estes Park, Colorado within Rocky Mountain National Park! This beautiful lake is surrounded by gorgeous mountain views and small islands that can be explored on foot or rented boats available at the lake during the summer months. In addition, you can take pictures of local wildlife such as sandhill cranes, osprey, elk, or moose near the shoreline.

Location: 89CR+6M Estes Park, Colorado

Closest City or Town: Estes Park, Colorado

How to Get There: Take US-34 W from downtown Estes Park towards Moraine Avenue for 4 miles until you reach Bear Lake Road. Turn left onto Bear Lake Rd and follow it until you see signs for the Sprague Lake parking area on your left side (3.4 mile).

GPS Coordinates: 40.3205625° N, 105.6083125° W

Best Time to Visit: Summer months are the best time for visiting as temperatures tend to be milder during that season

Pass/Permit/Fees: Entrance fees vary depending on the activities. Please visit their website for more details.

Did you Know? Sprague Lake is a great spot for fishing as it is stocked with rainbow, brook, and brown trout in the summer months!

Website: http://www.nps.gov/romo

Bear Lake Trailhead

Embark on your journey to Bear Lake Trailhead, located in Estes Park, Colorado within Rocky Mountain National Park! This trailhead provides access to many of the beautiful trails of the park including Alberta Falls and Emerald Lake Trail. Along with picturesque views of forests and mountain peaks, you can also expect to see wildlife like moose, elk, or osprey while hiking along the trails.

Location: Bear Lake Rd, Estes Park, CO 80517

Closest City or Town: Estes Park, Colorado

How to Get There: Take US-34 W from downtown Estes Park towards Moraine Avenue for 4 miles until you reach Bear Lake Road. Turn left onto Bear Lake Rd and follow it until you see signs for Bear Lake Trailhead on your left side (1.6 mile).

GPS Coordinates: 40.3483831° N, 105.577299° W

Best Time to Visit: Summer months are the best time for visiting as temperatures tend to be milder during that season

Pass/Permit/Fees: Entrance fees vary depending on the activities. Please visit their website for more details.

Did you Know? The Bear Lake Trailhead is located close to the Bear Lake shuttle stop, making it easily accessible for visitors!

Website:
https://www.nps.gov/romo/planyourvisit/list_hiking_trails.htm

Lily Lake

Located in the Rocky Mountain National Park, Lily Lake is a tranquil spot surrounded by beautiful wildflowers and stunning views of Longs Peak. Enjoy kayaking or fishing on the lake or birdwatching along its shores. Venture up to the summit for spectacular panoramic vistas of Estes Valley before settling down to camp under an endless sky of stars.

Location: Estes Park, CO 80517

Closest City or Town: Estes Park, Colorado

How to Get There: From US Hwy 36 in Estes Park head south on MacGregor Ave until you reach Lily Lake Rd. Follow it around until you reach the lake.

GPS Coordinates: 40.3772059° N, 105.5216651° W

Best Time to Visit: Summer and Fall are best for outdoor activities at this destination

Pass/Permit/Fees: Entrance fees may apply depending on activities ($20)

Did you Know? Lily Lake is recognized as one of the best places in Rocky Mountain National Park for spotting moose.

Website: https://www.nps.gov/romo/lily_lake.htm

Alluvial Fan

Discover an ancient geological wonder at the Alluvial Fan, located in Rocky Mountain National Park. This impressive landscape of sedimentary rocks was formed after a catastrophic flood in 1982 and is now home to many forms of wildlife. Follow the walking trails to explore this unique area and take in its stunning beauty with panoramic views of Longs Peak and Mt Meeker.

Location: Alluvial Fan Trail, Estes Park, CO 80517

Closest City or Town: Estes Park, Colorado

How to Get There: From US Hwy 36 take CO-7 N/CO-66 W until you reach MacGregor Ave. Follow it to the Alluvial Fan Trail, then take a left where you will see signs for the Alluvial Fan.

GPS Coordinates: 40.4107054° N, 105.6348631° W

Best Time to Visit: Summer and Fall are best for outdoor activities at this destination

Pass/Permit/Fees: Entrance fees may apply depending on activities ($20)

Did you Know? Scientists believe that the rocks found in this area originated from glaciers located forty miles away!

Website: https://www.usgs.gov/

Website: https://www.usgs.gov/media/images/alluvial-fan-rocky-mountain-national-park

Peak to Peak Scenic Byway

Embark on a journey of discovery along Colorado's breathtaking Peak-to-Peak Scenic Byway. This picturesque route is the highest continuous highway in the state, with stunning views of snowcapped mountains and wildflower meadows that will take your breath away.

Drive past peaceful lakeside towns and expansive forests as you traverse nearly 55 miles of mountain roads.

Location: 72 CO-7, Estes Park, CO 80517

Closest City or Town: Estes Park, Colorado

How to Get There: From US Hwy 36 take-7 N/CO-66 W until you reach the starting point of the highway

GPS Coordinates: 40.3752181° N, 105.5095565° W

Best Time to Visit: Summer and Fall are best for outdoor activities along this route

Pass/Permit/Fees: Entrance fees may apply depending on activities ($20)

Did you Know? This highway is one of the longest and highest continuous highways in Colorado, spanning nearly 55 miles.

Website: https://www.codot.gov/travel/scenic-byways/north-central/peak-to-peak

Estes Park Visitor Center

Explore the wild and wonderful wonders of Estes Park at the Estes Park Visitor Center. With over 300 miles of trails, visitors can spend days in stunning natural surroundings and discover hidden gems like cascading waterfalls, mountain peaks, and alpine lakes. The visitor center also offers educational programs to explore the area's unique history and culture, as well as guided tours for a more immersive experience.

Location: 500 Big Thompson Ave, Estes Park, CO 80517-9649

Closest City or Town: Estes Park, Colorado

How to Get There: From US Hwy 36 take MacGregor Ave until you reach Big Thompson Ave. Turn right and follow it to the Estes Park Visitor Center.

GPS Coordinates: 40.3788018° N, 105.5142382° W

Best Time to Visit: Summer and Fall are best for outdoor activities in Estes Park

Pass/Permit/Fees: Free

Did you Know? Estes Park was named after Missouri native Joel Estes, who came to the area in 1859.

Website: http://estespark.colorado.gov/visitorservices/

Lake Estes Marina

Take a break from the hustle and bustle of everyday life by visiting Lake Estes Marina in Colorado. Located on Big Thompson Avenue in beautiful Estes Park, this marina offers a variety of recreational activities such as fishing, canoeing, kayaking, and paddleboarding. Take on the beauty of nature while exploring the tranquil waters and stunning mountain views that surround you. You can also rent boats or fishing gear if needed for your adventure on the lake!

Location: 1770 Big Thompson Ave, Estes Park, CO 80517-8928

Closest City or Town: Estes Park (located within)

How to Get There: Take US-34 E/Big Thompson Ave until you reach 1770 Big Thompson Ave for directions to the marina entrance

GPS Coordinates: 40.3786827° N, 105.4918037° W

Best Time to Visit: Visiting during spring or fall is ideal as temperatures tend to be milder **Pass/Permit/Fees:** Various fees apply depending on activities

Did you Know? The lake was formed when an earthen dam was built across the Big Thompson River back in 1901

Website : http://evrpd.colorado.gov/lake-estes-marina

Snowy Peaks Winery

Experience one of Colorado's finest wineries at Snowy Peaks Winery in Estes Park. Relax and enjoy a glass of their award-winning wines in the stunning views of nature as you tour the vineyards and production facility. Enjoy learning about the wine-making process while sampling some of their signature varietals such as Chardonnay, Pinot Noir, Sangiovese, and Cabernet Sauvignon.

Location: 292 Moraine Ave, Estes Park, CO 80517

Closest City or Town: Estes Park (located within)

How to Get There: Take US-36 W until you reach Moraine Ave for directions to Snowy Peaks Winery entrance

GPS Coordinates: 40.3731896° N, 105.523396° W

Best Time to Visit: The winery is open year-round and has outdoor seating so visitors can enjoy the views of the vineyards while tasting their wines

Pass/Permit/Fees: Wine tastings are available for a fee (prices vary)

Did you Know? Snowy Peaks Winery was named after the 13,000 ft peaks of Rocky Mountain National Park which is just minutes away

Website: http://www.snowypeakswinery.com/

EVERGREEN

Evergreen Lake

Escape to Evergreen Lake in Colorado and embark on an adventure of a lifetime! Offering spectacular mountain views, this lake is perfect for fishing, boating, kayaking, and stand-up paddleboarding. Spend a day exploring the lake's picturesque shoreline or hike one of the nearby trails for breathtaking views of nature.

Location: 29612 Upper Bear Creek Rd, Evergreen, CO 80439

Closest City or Town: Evergreen (located within)

How to Get There: Take I-70W until you reach US-40 West. Then take US-74 South/Evergreen Parkway until you reach Upper Bear Creek Rd for directions to Evergreen Lake entrance

GPS Coordinates: 39.6315957° N, 105.3311845° W

Best Time to Visit: The lake is open year-round with moderate temperatures during spring and fall being the best time to visit

Pass/Permit/Fees: Entrance fees apply (prices vary)

Did you Know? Evergreen Lake is one of the oldest natural recreation areas in Colorado, having been used since the late 1800s by local residents for fishing, picnicking, and boating.

Website: http://www.evergreenrecreation.com/

FAIRPLAY

South Park City Museum

Discover a unique piece of Colorado's history at the South Park City Museum in Fairplay! This museum was built to look like an authentic gold mining town from the 19th century with over 3 million artifacts on display throughout its buildings. Learn about life during this era through interactive exhibits as you explore historic buildings such as a blacksmith shop, schoolhouse, and saloon.

Location: 100 4th St, Fairplay, CO 80440-9903

Closest City or Town: Fairplay (located within)

How to Get There: Take US-285 N/US-160 W until you reach 4th St for directions to South Park City Museum entrance

GPS Coordinates: 39.2252087° N, 106.0036827° W

Best Time to Visit: Summer is the best time to visit due to the mild temperatures **Pass/Permit/Fees:** Entrance fees apply (prices vary)

Did you Know? South Park City Museum was built in 1959 to preserve the artifacts of South Park City and pay respect to its residents who lived there during the 19th century

Website: http://southparkcity.org/

FORT COLLINS

New Belgium Brewing

Discover the taste of craft beer at New Belgium Brewing in Fort Collins, Colorado. With a taproom located in an old sugar beet factory, this brewery offers visitors a unique experience for sampling their famous Fat Tire and other world-class brews. From interactive tours to special events like yoga classes where you can sample beers afterward - there's something exciting for everyone here! Located just off Linden Street, it's the perfect spot to grab a cold one with friends or family.

Location: 500 Linden St, Fort Collins, CO 80524-2457

Closest City or Town: Fort Collins, Colorado

How to Get There: Take Lincoln Avenue south until you reach Linden Street and turn left; the brewery is on your right side.

GPS Coordinates: 40.5931253° N, 105.0679797° W

Best Time to Visit: Anytime! The taproom is open year-round from 11am – 7pm Mon-Thurs and 10am – 6pm Fri & Sat (closed Sun).

Pass/Permit/Fees: None required unless noted otherwise for special events.

Did you Know? New Belgium has won more awards than any other American craft brewery at the Great American Beer Festival.

Website: http://www.newbelgium.com/visit/fort-collins/

Horsetooth Mountain Open Space

Take in sweeping views of the Front Range at Horsetooth Mountain Open Space, a 6,711-acre park just west of Fort Collins, Colorado. Explore over 50 miles of trails with challenging rock formations or relax by one of two crystal clear reservoirs – Horsetooth and Soderberg Lakes. There's plenty to do here no matter your skill level - from easy jaunts along paths to serious hikes up steep inclines and horseback riding!

Location: 6550 W County Rd 38 E, Fort Collins, CO 80526

Closest City or Town: Fort Collins, Colorado

How to Get There: Take US-287 N, then turn left onto W County Rd 38E. Follow the signs for Horsetooth Mountain Open Space.

GPS Coordinates: 40.5237253° N, 105.1811812° W

Best Time to Visit: Spring and fall are best as temperatures tend to be milder during those seasons; however, the park is open year-round from 6am – 10pm daily (9pm in winter).

Pass/Permit/Fees: None required unless noted otherwise for special events.

Did you Know? The distinctive ridge of this mountain range was created when molten lava cooled and eroded during the Ice Age.

Website: http://www.larimer.org/parks/htmp.cfm

Odell Brewing Company

Sample a variety of craft beers at Odell Brewing Company in Fort Collins, Colorado. This family-run brewery offers fun tours where you can learn about beer making and sample them afterward with your very own tasting glass! With an emphasis on sustainability, Odell takes care to minimize its environmental footprint while crafting some of the best beers around - from IPAs to stouts and crisp ales. Whether you're a beer enthusiast or just looking for something new to try, there's something for everyone here!

Location: 800 E Lincoln Ave, Fort Collins, CO 80524-2507

Closest City or Town: Fort Collins, Colorado

How to Get There: Take Lincoln Avenue east until you reach the brewery on your right.

GPS Coordinates: 40.5894796° N, 105.0633306° W

Best Time to Visit: Tour times vary depending on the day; check their website for more information on specific times and availability.

Pass/Permit/Fees: None required unless noted otherwise for special events.

Did you Know? Odell was recently recognized as having one of the top five tap rooms in America by USA TODAY!

Website: http://odellbrewing.com/

FRISCO

Frisco Adventure Park

Set your sights on some of the best skiing and snowboarding in Colorado at Frisco Adventure Park. This family-friendly destination located just northwest of Denver offers a wealth of winter activities including tubing, Nordic skiing, ice skating, sleigh rides, and more! With trails for all skill levels, you can explore nature or test your skill at one of the terrain parks - it's up to you!

Location: 621 Recreation Way, Frisco, CO 80443

Closest City or Town: Frisco, Colorado

How to Get There: Take I-70 W until you reach Exit 203; turn right onto Highway 9 southbound for approximately three miles. Then take a left onto Recreation Way and the Park will be on your right.

GPS Coordinates: 39.5741089° N, 106.0776579° W

Best Time to Visit: Wintertime is best for snow-based activities, however, there are plenty of other things to do all year round and the park typically opens in mid-October.

Pass/Permit/Fees: Entrance fees vary depending on activity; check the website for more information.

Did you Know? The Frisco Nordic Center is home to Colorado's only dog sledding team!

Website: http://www.townoffrisco.com/adventure-park/

Frisco Historic Park and Museum

Travel back in time to the vibrant old mining town of Frisco. Explore historic buildings, stroll through the streets lined with colorful Victorian-era storefronts, and learn about local history at the interactive museum. Located along Main Street in downtown Frisco, this is an ideal destination for anyone who loves learning about history or simply wants to take a step back into Colorado's past.

Location: 120 Main Street, Frisco, CO 80443

Closest City or Town: Frisco, Colorado (located within the city)

How to Get There: From Summit Boulevard/US-6 drive east on 2nd Ave until you reach Main St., then turn right onto Main St until reaching your destination

GPS Coordinates: 39.5754814° N, 106.1005646° W

Best Time to Visit: Open year-round but summer months are best for exploring comfortably

Pass/Permit/Fees: Entrance is free

Did you Know? The park features two original log cabins built during the 1870s when silver was discovered nearby!

Website: http://www.townoffrisco.com/activities/historic-park-museum/

GEORGETOWN

Loveland Ski Area

Grab your skis and snowboard and hit the slopes at Loveland Ski Area! Located just off I-70 in Georgetown, Colorado, this ski resort offers thrilling winter fun for all ages. Enjoy a variety of terrain from gentle beginner trails to extreme runs for experienced riders or take a break with hot chocolate and snacks at one of the cozy lodges. Whether you're an expert or novice, come experience the thrilling rush of adrenaline that only skiing can offer!

Location: I-70 Exit 216, Georgetown, CO 80435

Closest City or Town: Georgetown, Colorado (just a short drive away)

How to Get There: From I-70 take Exit 216, follow the signs to Loveland Ski Area, and enjoy the scenic drive up

GPS Coordinates: 39.7184198° N, 105.6962957° W

Best Time to Visit: Winter months (December to March) are best for skiing

Pass/Permit/Fees: Lift tickets vary depending on age group and type of pass ($50-$90). Please visit their website for more details.

Did you Know? Loveland Ski Area is one of Colorado's oldest ski resorts! It opened in 1936 with three rope tows and several trails.

Website: http://www.skiloveland.com/

Guanella Pass

Whether you're an avid hiker or a nature lover, Guanella Pass will satisfy your thirst for outdoor adventure. This scenic byway stretches across the Continental Divide in the Rocky Mountains, offering breathtaking views and unforgettable experiences. Along the way, you can spot wildlife such as elk and marmots, take in amazing panoramic views of the mountains, and admire wildflowers blooming in late summer.

Location: Colorado 80435

Closest City or Town: Georgetown, Colorado (just 10 miles away)

How to Get There: From I-70 take Exit 228 (Georgetown/Silver Plume exit), then head south on State Hwy 103 until reaching your destination

GPS Coordinates: 39.6007426° N, 105.8525154° W

Best Time to Visit: Summer and fall months are best for enjoying the outdoors

Pass/Permit/Fees: No entrance fees or passes required

Did you Know? Guanella Pass is named in honor of an early pioneer who ran a stage station at this spot!

Website: http://www.coloradodot.info/travel/scenic-byways/north-central/guanella-pass

Capital Prize Gold Mine Tour

Step back into Colorado's gold rush era with a visit to the Capital Prize Gold Mine tour in Georgetown. This hands-on experience takes you deep underground, where you can explore old mine tunnels and learn about the area's rich mining history. Above ground, take a look at the original equipment and buildings used during the gold rush days. It's an educational experience that's sure to captivate kids and adults alike!

Location: 1016 Biddle Street, Georgetown, CO 80444

Closest City or Town: Georgetown, Colorado (just steps away)

How to Get There: From I-70 take Exit 228 (Georgetown/Silver Plume exit), then head south on State Hwy 103 until reaching your destination

GPS Coordinates: 39.7095713° N, 105.6924298° W

Best Time to Visit: Open year-round but summer months are best for exploring comfortably

Pass/Permit/Fees: Adults (ages 13+) $10.00, Kids (Ages 5-12) $5.00

Did you Know? The Capital Prize Gold Mine operated here from 1877 to 1942 and produced an impressive total of 6 million ounces of gold during that time!

Website: http://www.capitalprizegoldmine.com/

GLENWOOD SPRINGS

Hanging Lake Trail

Discover the beauty of the Rocky Mountains at Hanging Lake Trail, a picturesque destination nestled deep in Glenwood Canyon. Popular among hikers and nature lovers alike, this enchanting spot is home to stunning waterfalls, rocky cliffs, lush foliage, and a crystal-clear lake suspended along an overhanging cliffside. From the top of the trail, you can take in sweeping views of mountains and valleys as far as your eyes can see – it's no wonder why this place has become such an iconic Colorado landmark! Take on the 1.2-mile hike with caution; though well worth it for those willing to make it all the way up for one of life's most majestic experiences.

Location: 70 East County Rd 125, Glenwood Springs CO 81601

Closest City or Town: Glenwood Springs, Colorado (located within the city)

How to Get There: Take I-70 east until you reach Exit 124 onto County Road 125 towards Hanging Lake Waypoint Signage/Trailhead

GPS Coordinates: 39.5563108° N, 107.336453° W

Best Time to Visit: Summer months are best for visiting but due to its popularity, the trail can get crowded.

Pass/Permit/Fees: There is a $10 fee to access the trailhead for adults and kids under 16 are free.

Did you Know? Hanging Lake is home to several endangered species of fish, as well as rare wildflowers found only at this location.

Website: http://visitglenwood.com/things-to-do/hanging-lake

Glenwood Caverns Adventure Park

Challenge yourself on thrilling rides, explore secret passages in a historic cave tour, or take in breathtaking views from atop Iron Mountain – Glenwood Caverns Adventure Park has something for everyone! Located just outside of Glenwood Springs, Colorado, this family-friendly park is full of adventure and exploration. Take a trip to the top of Iron Mountain via the Giant Canyon Swing, explore the mysterious Fairy Caves with over 400 million years of history beneath your feet, or try the thrilling Haunted Mine Drop! No matter what you choose, Glenwood Caverns Adventure Park will be an experience like no other.

Location: 51000 Two Rivers Plaza Rd, Glenwood Springs CO 81601-2809

Closest City or Town: Glenwood Springs, Colorado (just a short drive away)

How to Get There: From downtown Flagstaff take I-70 W until you reach Exit 116 onto 6th Street in Glenwood Springs. Follow 6th Street for two miles until you reach Two Rivers Plaza Rd on your left.

GPS Coordinates: 39.5563108° N, 107.336453° W

Best Time to Visit: Glenwood Caverns Adventure Park is open from May-September and hours vary by season, check the website for more information!

Pass/Permit/Fees: Prices depend on individual activities and attractions but all-day passes are available; visit their website for more details.

Did you Know? The park is home to the world's highest elevation maze, located at an elevation of 7,160 ft!

Website: http://www.glenwoodcaverns.com/

Glenwood Vaudeville Revue

The Glenwood Vaudeville Revue is one of the longest-running variety shows in Colorado! Located in the heart of Glenwood Springs, this two-hour dinner show is filled with music, comedy, and dance that will leave you enthralled. Experience a unique blend of classic vaudeville acts and modern musical numbers as talented performers take you through a journey full of laughter, excitement, and entertainment. Enjoy an evening out for all ages – make sure to get there early to enjoy drinks at the bar before the show begins!

Location: 915 Grand Ave Springs Theatre, Glenwood Springs CO 81601-3601

Closest City or Town: Glenwood Springs, Colorado (located within the city)

How to Get There: Take I-70 east until you reach Exit 116 onto 6th Street in Glenwood Springs. Follow 6th Street for two miles until you reach Grand Ave on your left.

GPS Coordinates: 39.5447581° N, 107.325154° W

Best Time to Visit: The show runs annually from June - September and tickets must be purchased in advance online or by phone.

Pass/Permit/Fees: Prices vary depending on show times and seating options, visit their website for more details.

Did you Know? This long-running variety show is the only one of its kind west of the Mississippi River!

Website: http://www.gvrshow.com/

Sunlight Mountain Resort

Located in the Rocky Mountains of Colorado, Sunlight Mountain Resort offers an unforgettable outdoor adventure. From skiing and snowboarding during winter months to mountain biking and hiking in summer, this resort has something for everyone. Whether you're a beginner or an expert-level skier or boarder, take your pick from 48 unique trails that range from bunny slopes to challenging terrain parks! With plenty of apres ski options like restaurants and bars, take in the breathtaking views while enjoying delicious local fare.

Location: 10901 County Road 117, Glenwood Springs, CO 81601-4541

Closest City or Town: Glenwood Springs

How to Get There: Head northeast on I-70 E until you reach Exit 116 (Glenwood Springs/Hwy 82 W). Follow HWY 82 W for 2 miles before turning left onto Midland Ave., then turn right at N River St. Turn left onto 6th St followed by another left onto Castle Creek Rd., where you will continue for 4 miles until reaching County Road 117 towards Sunlight Mountain Resort.

GPS Coordinates: 39.3996715° N, 107.3385376° W

Best Time to Visit: Winter months from November to March offers the best ski conditions.

Pass/Permit/Fees: Ski passes and rental fees vary depending on age, duration, and type of activity. Please visit their website for more details.

Did you Know? Sunlight Mountain Resort is the closest ski area to Aspen!

Website: http://www.sunlightmtn.com/

GOLDEN

Lookout Mountain

High above the city of Golden lies Lookout Mountain, a beautiful mountain park with stunning views of Clear Creek Valley and Denver's skyline. This popular outdoor destination offers plenty of recreational activities such as horseback riding, hiking trails, camping sites, scenic drives, and beautiful picnic areas. Take in panoramic views from Buffalo Bill's grave at the top or explore the surrounding hills on a peaceful hike and take in the stunning rock formations.

Location: PQM6+59 Lakota Hills, Golden, Colorado

Closest City or Town: Golden, Colorado

How to Get There: Take I-70 W until you reach exit 256 (Lookout Mountain Road). Follow Lookout Mountain Rd for 3 miles before turning right onto Buffalo Bill Ct., which will lead you to the entrance of Lookout Mountain Park.

GPS Coordinates: 39.7329375° N, 105.2390625° W

Best Time to Visit: Spring and summer months are best for outdoor activities such as hiking and biking while winter is great for snowshoeing or cross-country skiing.

Pass/Permit/Fees: Entrance to the park is free, however, fees may apply for certain activities such as horseback riding ($5-$30). Please visit their website for more details.

Did you Know? Lookout Mountain is home to Buffalo Bill's grave and a museum that chronicles his life!

Website: http://www.buffalobill.org/

Golden Gate Canyon State Park

Located in the forested foothills of Colorado's Front Range, Golden Gate Canyon State Park offers an outdoor playground of hiking trails, camping sites, picnic areas, and scenic drives. This 12,000-acre park has something for everyone – take a peaceful stroll along the trails or explore the wildlife of the area. Enjoy picturesque views from the

Panorama Point Scenic Overlook or take in a fascinating historical tour of the Golden Gate Canyon Historic District.

Location: 3873 Highway 46 92 Crawford Gulch Road, Golden, CO 80403

Closest City or Town: Golden, Colorado

How to Get There: From I-70 Westbound, take Exit 254 (Coot Hill/CO 93). Turn right onto CO 93 and follow for 8 miles before turning left onto County Rd 72. Take another left onto Arapahoe Rd and continue until you reach Hwy 46. Follow this road for 3 miles until you reach the park entrance on your left.

GPS Coordinates: 39.755543° N, 105.2210997° W

Best Time to Visit: Spring and Fall are great times of the year for visiting Golden Gate Canyon State Park as the weather is milder compared to summer months. Winters can get quite cold so make sure to dress accordingly if visiting during this time.

Pass/Permit/Fees: A Colorado State Parks Pass ($7 daily/$70 annually) is required for entrance into the park. Please visit their website for more details on prices and fees.

Did you Know? This state park offers up over 38 miles of trails for visitors to explore!

Website:
http://cpw.state.co.us/placestogo/parks/GoldenGateCanyon

Colorado School of Mines Geology Museum

Explore the depths of geological history at the Colorado School of Mines Geology Museum. Home to a vast collection of rocks, minerals, and fossils from across the world, this museum is sure to fascinate! Take a guided tour to learn about the various specimens on display or explore the interactive exhibits that showcase gems, fossils, and meteorites from around the globe.

Location: 1310 Maple St, Golden, CO 80401-1800

Closest City or Town: Golden, Colorado

How to Get There: Head westbound on I-70 until you reach Exit 259 (Maple Street). Turn left onto 15th St before turning right onto Maple Street where you will reach the museum on your left.

GPS Coordinates: 39.7517046° N, 105.2250338° W

Best Time to Visit: The museum is open year-round from Monday-Friday 9AM-4PM with extended hours during summer months (May-August).

Pass/Permit/Fees: Admission to the museum is free for all visitors.

Did you Know? This museum is home to one of the world's largest collections of dinosaur bones!

Website: https://geologymuseum.mines.edu/

GRAND JUNCTION

Colorado National Monument

Discover the magnificent beauty of Colorado's rugged landscape at the Colorado National Monument. Located in western Colorado, this national park is home to a diverse array of wildlife and plant life amid its spectacular red rock canyons and towering sandstone mesas. Enjoy breathtaking views from one of the scenic overlooks or explore the trails on foot for a closer look at nature's wonders. Take an unforgettable ride along Rim Rock Drive—carved into the sheer cliffs many years ago—to marvel at this extraordinary place!

Location: 1750 Rim Rock Dr, Fruita, CO 81521

Closest City or Town: Grand Junction, Colorado

How to Get There: From downtown Grand Junction take I-70 W towards Fruita/Palisade then take Exit 19 onto CO-340 E until you reach Monument Rd W. Turn left onto Monument Rd W followed by a right turn onto Rim Rock Dr N towards the visitor center entrance.

GPS Coordinates: 38.9826089° N, 108.5938124° W

Best Time to Visit: Open year-round but spring (March to May) has more moderate temperatures so it may be more comfortable for outdoor activities like hiking trails around that time.

Pass/Permit/Fees: Entrance to the park is free but there may be fees for camping and other recreational activities.

Did you Know? This national monument was originally named the Colorado National Canyon in 1906 by President Theodore Roosevelt but changed its name in 1911.

Website: http://www.nps.gov/colm/index.htm

Grand Mesa

Take a journey of discovery at Grand Mesa, the world's largest flat-top mountain standing tall over Western Colorado's rolling hills and valleys. Spanning over 500 square miles, this spectacular natural formation features crystal-clear alpine lakes, lush forests, and extensive trails perfect for exploring! The area is also renowned as one of the best places for skiing in the state, with numerous ski resorts and winter activities.

Location: Colorado Highway 65 20090 Baron Lake Drive, Grand Junction, CO 81413

Closest City or Town: Grand Junction, Colorado

How to Get There: From downtown Grand Junction take I-70 W until you reach Exit 49 onto CO-65 S/Mesa Lakes Rd towards Mesa Lakes Resort. Turn right onto CO-65 S/Baron Lake Dr and follow signs to the area.

GPS Coordinates: 39.0638705° N, 108.5506486° W

Best Time to Visit: The best time to visit is during the summer months when temperatures are milder making it more enjoyable for outdoor recreation.

Pass/Permit/Fees: Entrance to the park is free but there may be fees for camping and other recreational activities.

Did you Know? Grand Mesa has over 300 lakes and multiple species of wildlife including elk, moose, coyotes, bald eagles, and more!

Website:
http://www.fs.usda.gov/recarea/gmug/recarea/?recid=32942

Downtown Grand Junction

Experience the charm and vibrancy of Downtown Grand Junction! This vibrant area offers a myriad of exciting attractions perfect for visitors of all ages such as monuments, museums, galleries & theaters that bring this city's rich history to life. Quench your thirst for adventure with thrilling outdoor activities like kayaking, biking, and hiking the nearby trails, or just linger in one of the many pubs and restaurants to take in this city's lively atmosphere.

Location: 541 Main St, Grand Junction, CO 81501

Closest City or Town: Grand Junction, Colorado

How to Get There: From I-70 W/E, exit onto N 6th St until you reach Main St. Turn left onto Main Street and follow signs to the Downtown Grand Junction area.

GPS Coordinates: 39.0670015° N, 108.5633616° W

Best Time to Visit: The best time to visit is during the summer months when temperatures are milder making it more enjoyable for outdoor recreation.

Pass/Permit/Fees: Entrance to the park is free but there may be fees for camping and other recreational activities.

Did you Know? Downtown Grand Junction has been designated as a "Colorado Creative District" due to the area's unique local arts scene!

Website: http://www.downtowngj.org/

GRAND LAKE

Alpine Visitor Center

Take in breathtaking views of Rocky Mountain National Park at the Alpine Visitor Center, perched high atop Trail Ridge Road. This stunning location offers spectacular alpine scenery - from snow-covered mountains to lush meadows and wildflowers – perfect for capturing those postcard-ready moments! Here you can explore the area on foot, take a ranger-led tour or just relax and enjoy the tranquil beauty of nature.

Location: Trail Ridge Rd, Grand Lake, CO 80447

Closest City or Town: Grand Lake, Colorado

How to Get There: From Grand Lake take US Highway 34 towards Estes Park then turn right onto Trail Ridge Rd. Continue for several miles until you reach the visitor center entrance.

GPS Coordinates: 40.2542527° N, 105.8351567° W

Best Time to Visit: The best time to visit is during the summer months when temperatures are milder making it more enjoyable for outdoor recreation.

Pass/Permit/Fees: Entrance to the park is free but there may be fees for camping and other recreational activities.

Did you Know? This visitor center sits at an elevation of 11,796 ft making it one of the highest drives in the country!

Website:https://www.nps.gov/romo/planyourvisit/alpine_visitor_center.htm

IDAHO SPRINGS

Argo Mill and Tunnel

Explore the hallowed grounds of one of Colorado's oldest historical attractions, the Argo Mill and Tunnel. Located in Idaho Springs just a short drive from Denver, visitors will find an array of old mining equipment, jaw-dropping views of the Clear Creek canyon, and a fascinating tour of the historic mill itself. Camping is also available for those who wish to experience this unusual slice of history up close!

Location: 2350 Riverside Drive, Idaho Springs, CO 80452

Closest City or Town: Idaho Springs

How to Get There: From Denver follow I-70 E until you reach Exit 240 (Fall River Rd). Follow Fall River Rd north until it intersects with Riverside Dr., then turn left onto Riverside Dr to arrive at Argo Mill & Tunnel.

GPS Coordinates: 39.7426527° N, 105.5060195° W

Best Time to Visit: Summers are mild in this part of Colorado but avoid visiting during peak snowmelt season when floods along Clear Creek can cause dangerous conditions. **Pass/Permit/Fees:** Admission costs $15 per person; camping is available for an additional fee ($20-$30).

Did you Know? The mill was built in 1913 after gold ore was discovered nearby by prospectors back in 1859!

Website: http://www.argomilltour.com/

St. Mary's Glacier

Stand in awe of the stunning St. Mary's Glacier located in the Arapaho National Forest just outside of Idaho Springs. Enjoy a wide array of recreational activities such as fishing, camping, and hiking on nearby trails with views overlooking the glacier lake. This is also an ideal spot for wintertime fun with snowshoeing and sledding available during the colder months!

Location: 7599 Fall River Road, Idaho Springs, CO 80452

Closest City or Town: Idaho Springs

How to Get There: From Denver take I-70 E until you reach Exit 240 (Fall River Rd). Turn right onto Fall River Rd and keep going until you see signs for St. Mary's Lake.

GPS Coordinates: 39.8095467° N, 105.6394148° W

Best Time to Visit: Summers are the best time of year to visit as temperatures tend to be milder during that season and snow will have melted off most trails.

Pass/Permit/Fees: Entrance is free, however, campers must pay the appropriate fees ($20-$30).

Did you Know? This area was once home to prospectors who were drawn here by rumors of gold in this frozen land!

Website:
http://www.fs.usda.gov/recarea/arp/recreation/recarea/?recid=83419&actid=50

KEENESBURG

Wild Animal Sanctuary

Discover the wonders of wildlife at Wild Animal Sanctuary, one of the largest carnivore sanctuaries in the world. Here, visitors will find over 500 rescued animals from all around the globe living in spacious natural habitats with plenty of room to roam. Enjoy educational tours as you explore this incredible refuge and learn more about these majestic creatures!

Location: 2999 County Road 53, Keenesburg, CO 80643-4209

Closest City or Town: Keenesburg

How to Get There: From Denver take I-76 E until Exit 47 (Keenesburg). Turn left onto State Highway 52 N for several miles before turning right onto County Rd 53 to arrive at Wild Animal Sanctuary.

GPS Coordinates: 40.0438138° N, 104.5653621° W

Best Time to Visit: Anytime of the year is a good time to visit as temperatures in this part of Colorado tend to be milder during both summer and winter months.

Pass/Permit/Fees: Admission costs $20 per person.

Did you Know? This sanctuary is home to some of the world's most endangered species including tigers, lions, and bears!

Website: http://www.wildanimalsanctuary.org/

KEYSTONE

Arapahoe Basin

Take your adventure to Arapahoe Basin, the premier ski resort of Colorado. Located along US Highway 6 in Keystone, this picturesque mountain paradise offers some of the best skiing and snowboarding experiences in the country. Take a breathtaking ride up on North America's highest skiable elevation and explore its endless terrain for all levels of thrill-seekers! Whether you're an expert or just beginning to learn, there's something here for everyone. Enjoy stunning views of the Rocky Mountains throughout your winter wonderland adventure at Arapahoe Basin!

Location: 28194 US Hwy 6, Keystone, CO 80435

Closest City or Town: Keystone, Colorado (nearby)

How to Get There: From Denver take I-70 W/US-6 W until you reach Exit 205. Turn left onto Montezuma Rd., then right onto US-6 E where you will see signs pointing towards the Arapahoe Basin Ski Area entrance.

GPS Coordinates: 39.6423806° N, 105.8716948° W

Best Time to Visit: Winter season from November through April is the best time for skiing activities   **Pass/Permit/Fees:** Lift tickets and rentals vary in price. Please visit their website for more details.

Did you Know? Arapahoe Basin is home to the longest ski season in Colorado, with slopes open from October to late June!

Website: http://arapahoebasin.com/

La Junta

Bent's Old Fort National Historic Site

The iconic Bent's Old Fort National Historic Site preserves the legacy of this once bustling 19th-century fur trading post located on the banks of the Arkansas River in La Junta, Colorado. Wander through adobe walls and explore its many rooms filled with artifacts that bring to life a fascinating glimpse into frontier history. Visitors can also participate in special events such as Living History Days, where you can learn more about fur trade techniques and watch demonstrations of life in the 1840s.

Location: 35110 Colo. 194 E, La Junta, CO 81050

Closest City or Town: La Junta, Colorado (nearby)

How to Get There: From Denver take I-25 S until you reach Exit 74. Turn right onto US-350 W, then left onto Santa Fe Trail Scenic Byway/CO-194 E where you will see signs pointing towards Bent's Old Fort National Historic Site entrance.

GPS Coordinates: 38.0448514° N, 103.4340256° W

Best Time to Visit: Spring and fall seasons are the best time to visit the site due to mild temperatures **Pass/Permit/Fees:** Entrance fees are charged for adults ($3); children 15 and under are free. Please visit their website for more details.

Did you Know? The fort is unique in the western U.S., as it was built with a combination of Native American, Mexican, and European architectural styles!

Website: http://www.nps.gov/beol/index.htm

LEADVILLE

National Mining Hall of Fame & Museum

The National Mining Hall of Fame & Museum celebrates the history of mining by preserving artifacts and stories from past generations. Located in Leadville, Colorado, this interactive museum offers visitors an opportunity to learn more about the people, places, and technologies that have shaped the mining industry in America. Tour through the museum's many exhibits highlighting significant moments in history and discover artifacts as old as 130 million years!

Location: 120 W 9th St, Leadville, CO 80461-3403

Closest City or Town: Leadville, Colorado (nearby)

How to Get There: From Denver take I-70 W until you reach Exit 195. Turn left onto US-24 S/E 2nd St., then right onto Harrison Ave where you will see signs pointing towards National Mining Hall of Fame & Museum entrance.

GPS Coordinates: 39.2513811° N, 106.2940037° W

Best Time to Visit: Summer season is the best time for outdoor activities

Pass/Permit/Fees: Admission prices vary by age. Please visit their website for more details.

Did you Know? The museum features the world's largest object ever moved on wheels, a 12-foot gold ore bucket!

Website: http://www.mininghalloffame.org/

LITTLETON

Roxborough State Park

Experience nature at its best in Roxborough State Park, located just outside of Littleton, Colorado. This beautiful park offers stunning views of the majestic Rocky Mountains and diverse wildlife such as deer, coyotes, and red foxes. Take a walk along the trails and explore various types of terrain from grasslands to wooded hillsides. Enjoy a variety of outdoor activities and marvel at the beauty of the area's red sandstone formations.

Location: 4751 E Roxborough Dr, Littleton, CO 80125-9029

Closest City or Town: Littleton, Colorado (nearby)

How to Get There: From Denver take I-25 S until you reach Exit 184. Turn right onto W Lincoln Ave., then left onto Roxborough Dr where you will see signs pointing towards Roxborough State Park entrance.

GPS Coordinates: 39.4296738° N, 105.0691463° W

Best Time to Visit: Spring and fall seasons are the best time to visit due to mild temperatures **Pass/Permit/Fees:** Entrance fees are charged for adults ($8); children 15 and under are free. Please visit their website for more details.

Did you Know? Roxborough State Park is home to a variety of dinosaur fossils, including tracks from Allosaurus!

Website: http://cpw.state.co.us/placestogo/parks/Roxborough

LONGMONT

Left Hand Brewing Company

Located in Longmont, Colorado, the Left Hand Brewing Company is a must-visit destination for craft beer lovers. Enjoy one of their brewery tours to learn about the brewing process and sample some delicious local brews. Afterward, explore the tasting room where you can find plenty of unique beers on tap plus snacks like pretzels and freshly made popcorn. Tours are offered year-round so don't miss your chance to visit this popular spot!

Location: 1265 Boston Ave., Longmont, CO 80501-5809

Closest City or Town: Longmont, Colorado

How to Get There: From downtown Longmont take US 287 N/CO 56 W until you reach Kimbark St. Turn right onto Kimbark St., then left onto S Sunset St before taking a slight left onto Boston Ave E. The brewery will be on your left after turning into Boston Ave E.

GPS Coordinates: 40.1582861° N, 105.1150233° W

Best Time to Visit: Anytime year-round

Pass/Permit/Fees: No fees or permits are required for visiting the brewery

Did you Know? Left Hand Brewing Company was one of the first breweries in Colorado to bottle and distribute nitro beers!

Website: http://www.lefthandbrewing.com/

LOVELAND

Benson Park Sculpture Garden

Explore over 80 sculptures placed throughout 30 acres of lush gardens at the Benson Park Sculpture Garden in Loveland, Colorado. This picturesque park is a great way to admire incredible works of art while enjoying nature's beauty too! Wander around the outdoor galleries while admiring the sculptures, then relax by one of the ponds and take in the stunning views. This is a must-visit for art lovers!

Location: 1125 W 29th St., Loveland, CO 80538

Closest City or Town: Loveland, Colorado

How to Get There: From downtown Loveland take US 287 N/N Lincoln Ave until you reach W 29th St. Turn left onto W 29th St., and the park will be on your right after crossing over Taft Ave.

GPS Coordinates: 40.4224517° N, 105.0936742° W

Best Time to Visit: Anytime year-round

Pass/Permit/Fees: No fees or permits are required for visiting the park.

Did you Know? Benson Park was originally called the Loveland Art Park and has been home to many local and international sculptures since its opening in 1984!

Website: http://www.sculptureinthepark.org/

MANITOU SPRINGS

Cave of the Winds Mountain Park

Discover an underground world at Cave of the Winds Mountain Park in Manitou Springs, Colorado! This limestone cave is a fascinating labyrinth filled with hidden crevices, rock formations, and even a pickax-wielding miner! Take one of their guided tours to explore the depths of this subterranean wonderland - you won't regret it!

Location: 100 Cave of the Winds Rd., Manitou Springs, CO 80829

Closest City or Town: Manitou Springs, Colorado

How to Get There: From downtown Manitou Springs take US 24 W/Manitou Ave until you reach Cave of the Winds Rd. Turn right onto Cave of the Winds Rd., and the park will be on your left after turning onto Ruxton Ave.

GPS Coordinates: 38.8725916° N, 104.9201269° W

Best Time to Visit: Anytime year-round

Pass/Permit/Fees: Entrance fees are required for visiting the cave

Did you Know? The limestone walls in the cave were formed over a million years ago by water erosion!

Website: http://www.caveofthewinds.com/

Manitou Springs Incline

Take your adventure to the next level at the Manitou Springs Incline in Manitou Springs, Colorado! This rigorous hiking trail is a former cable car track that climbs nearly 2000 feet and offers spectacular views of the city below. Tackle the grueling incline for an unforgettable experience - you won't regret it!

Location: 444 Ruxton Ave., Manitou Springs, CO 80829

Closest City or Town: Manitou Springs, Colorado

How to Get There: From downtown Manitou Springs take US 24 W/Manitou Ave until you reach Ruxton Ave. Turn right onto Ruxton

Ave., and the park will be on your left after crossing over Cave of the Winds Rd.

GPS Coordinates: 38.8563521° N, 104.9301474° W

Best Time to Visit: Spring-Fall

Pass/Permit/Fees: A pass is required for accessing the trail

Did you Know? Manitou Springs Incline was constructed by the Manitou & Pike's Peak Railway Company in 1907!

Website: http://www.pikes-peak.com/want-climb-manitou-incline

MESA VERDE NATIONAL PARK

Long House

Discover the secrets of the Ancestral Puebloans at Long House, an ancient ruin located in Mesa Verde National Park near Mancos, Colorado. Built around 1200 AD by a people who had mastered stone architecture and engineering, this dwelling was once home to more than 60 families. Adventurers can explore its rooms and climb up into towers as they learn about the lives of these incredible ancestors.

Location: Long House Tram Rte., Mesa Verde National Park, CO 81330

Closest City or Town: Mancos, Colorado

How to Get There: From Mancos take County Rd G south for 16 miles until you reach W Village Dr. Turn left onto W Village Dr., then turn right when you reach Long House Tour Route 1/Tram Route Rd.

GPS Coordinates: 37.186845° N, 108.5358085° W

Best Time to Visit: Spring or fall are ideal times for visiting since temperatures tend to be milder during those seasons

Pass/Permit/Fees: Entrance fees vary depending on the activities planned ($5-$25). Please visit the

Did you Know? Long House is

Did you Know? The name "Long House" was given to this ruin because it is the longest dwelling in Mesa Verde.

Website: https://www.nps.gov/meve/planyourvisit/guided_activities.htm

Cliff Palace

Step into a lost world and explore Cliff Palace, one of the best-known cliff dwellings of the Ancient Puebloans in Mesa Verde National Park, Colorado. Built-in the 12th century, this dwelling includes 150 rooms and 23 kivas (ceremonial buildings) that still stand today with some structures reaching four stories high! Visitors can climb ladders up to inaccessible areas and observe fascinating details carved into walls that hold stories of days gone by.

Location: Cliff Palace Loop, Mesa Verde National Park, CO 81330

Closest City or Town: Mancos, Colorado

How to Get There: From Mancos take County Rd G south for 16 miles until you reach W Village Dr. Turn left onto W Village Dr., then turn right when you reach Cliff Palace Loop.

GPS Coordinates: 37.1704343° N, 108.4724794° W

Best Time to Visit: Spring or fall are ideal times for visiting since temperatures tend to be milder during those seasons

Pass/Permit/Fees: Entrance fees vary depending on activities ($15 - $20). Please visit their website for details

Did you Know? Cliff Palace is the largest cliff dwelling in North America, and its walls have stood for centuries.

Website: http://www.visitmesaverde.com/discover/points-of-interest/cliff-dwellings/cliff-palace.aspx

Balcony House

Explore the secrets of an ancient civilization at Balcony House, a 12th-century ruin located in Mesa Verde National Park in southwestern Colorado. This multi-story structure was built as a home by the Ancestral Puebloans who left details carved into its walls that still tell their stories today. Adventurers can climb ladders up to inaccessible areas and explore chambers, passages, and tunnels, as well as see artifacts left behind by its ancient inhabitants.

Location: Cliff Palace Loop, Colorado 81330

Closest City or Town: Mancos, Colorado

How to Get There: From Mancos take County Rd G south for 16 miles until you reach W Village Dr. Turn left onto W Village Dr., then turn right when you reach Cliff Palace Loop.

GPS Coordinates: 37.1704343° N, 108.4724794° W

Best Time to Visit: Spring or fall are ideal times for visiting since temperatures tend to be milder during those seasons

Pass/Permit/Fees: Entrance fees vary depending on activities ($15 - $20). Please visit their website for details

Did you Know? Balcony House is the only ruin in Mesa Verde where visitors can explore a Kiva.

Website:
http://www.nps.gov/meve/learn/historyculture/cd_balcony_house.htm

Spruce Tree House

Get lost in time at Spruce Tree House, a spectacular multi-story dwelling built by the Ancient Puebloans at Mesa Verde National Park near Mancos, Colorado. This structure was made up of more than 130 rooms and eight kivas (ceremonial buildings), some of which were four stories tall! Visitors can ascend ladders to inaccessible chambers and tunnels, explore ruins that have stood for centuries, and admire the intricate details carved into the walls that mark this incredible site.

Location: Mesa Verde National Park, CO 81330

Closest City or Town: Mancos, Colorado

How to Get There: From Mancos take County Rd G south for 16 miles until you reach W Village Dr. Turn left onto W Village Dr., then turn right when you reach Spruce Tree House Trailhead.

GPS Coordinates: 37.1837823° N, 108.4886935° W

Best Time to Visit: Spring or fall are ideal times for visiting since temperatures tend to be milder during those seasons

Pass/Permit/Fees: Entrance fees vary depending on activities ($15 - $20). Please visit their website for details

Did you Know? Spruce Tree House is the third-largest cliff dwelling in Mesa Verde and was considered to be the most inaccessible until it was excavated in 1921.

Website: http://www.nps.gov/meve/index.htm

Mesa Verde National Park

Described as a "unique cultural landscape," Mesa Verde National Park in Colorado is an archaeological wonder. Take a journey back thousands of years to explore the ancient cliff dwellings and learn about the culture of the Puebloan people who lived here from 600-1300 AD. Enjoy stunning views of canyons and mesas on hikes throughout the park, or catch free ranger programs offered during peak season. With its spectacular landscapes and rich history, Mesa Verde is sure to be a memorable experience.

Location: 6GJQ+87 Mesa Verde National Park, Colorado

Closest City or Town: Cortez, Colorado

How to Get There: From Cortez, take US-160 W/Main St. and follow the signs for Mesa Verde National Park.

How to Get There: From Monticello take UT-211 W towards US-191 N until you reach CO Hwy 145 S/Douglas Pass Rd which will take you straight into the park entrance.

GPS Coordinates: 37.2308125° N, 108.4618125° W

Best Time to Visit: Peak season runs from April through October with mild temperatures that make for great outdoor exploring!

Pass/Permit/Fees: Entrance fees are $15 per person or $25 for a seven-day pass.

Did you Know? Mesa Verde National Park was declared a World Heritage Site by the United Nations in 1978.

Website: https://www.nps.gov/meve/index.htm

Mesa Verde Visitor and Research Center

Situated in the heart of Mesa Verde National Park, the Visitor & Research Center offers visitors a chance to explore the area's cultural history. Discover hundreds of artifacts on display, including pottery, jewelry, and tools that were used by ancient Puebloans. Pick up an audio guide for a self-guided tour or join a ranger program for more in-depth information about the park's past. Make sure to stop by before heading out into the canyon!

Location: 35853 Road H.5, Mesa Verde National Park, CO 81328-9325

Closest City or Town: Cortez, Colorado

How to Get There: From Cortez, take US-160 W/Main St. and follow the signs for Mesa Verde National Park. Then take a left onto Hwy 41 and follow the signs for the Visitor & Research Center.

GPS Coordinates: 37.2308729° N, 108.4618335° W

Best Time to Visit: Peak season runs from April through October when temperatures are more mild and ranger programs are available for free!

Pass/Permit/Fees: Entrance fees vary depending on activities ($5-$30). Please visit their website for more details.

Did you Know? This research center was originally built as a tuberculosis hospital in 1895!

Website: http://www.nps.gov/meve/planyourvisit/meve_vc.htm

MONTROSE

Black Canyon Of The Gunnison National Park

From its steep, sheer cliffs to its wildlife-filled canyons, Black Canyon of the Gunnison National Park is an outdoor adventurer's paradise. Take a boat ride down the Gunnison River to explore the depths of the canyon or hike along remote trails for views of Painted Wall, North America's tallest vertical cliff. With over 80 miles of hiking trails and plenty of whitewater rafting opportunities, Black Canyon promises excitement for all!

Location: H7G5+59 Montrose, Colorado

Closest City or Town: Montrose, Colorado

How to Get There: From Montrose, take US-50 E until you reach the park entrance.

GPS Coordinates: 38.5754375° N, 107.7415625° W

Best Time to Visit: Summer is peak season and temperatures can reach 90 degrees during the day, so make sure to bring plenty of water!

Pass/Permit/Fees: Entrance fees are $15 per person or $25 for a seven-day pass.

Did you Know? A variety of wildlife including bighorn sheep, elk, and deer call this canyon home!

Website: http://www.nps.gov/blca/index.htm

Museum of the Mountain West

Delight in the stories and artifacts of Colorado's Western heritage at the Museum of the Mountain West. Located in Montrose, this museum offers a unique look into life during different eras from 1800-1900. Take a guided tour or explore on your own with their self-guided audio tour for an immersive experience. With over 100,000 artifacts and stories to uncover, you will be sure to find something interesting!

Location: 68169 Miami Rd, Montrose, CO 81401-9593

Closest City or Town: Montrose, Colorado

How to Get There: From Montrose take US-550 S/S Townsend Ave until you reach Miami Rd where you will find the museum just off the road.

GPS Coordinates: 38.4881031° N, 107.8137069° W

Best Time to Visit: The museum is open year-round, but hours may vary due to holidays and weather conditions. Please check their website for more details.

Pass/Permit/Fees: Admission fees are $10 per adult or $5 per student with an ID.

Did you Know? This museum houses one of the world's largest collections of cowboy spurs!

Website: http://www.museumofthemountainwest.org/

Red Rocks Park and Amphitheatre

Step into the breathtaking Red Rocks Park and Amphitheatre, an iconic venue located near Morrison, Colorado. Home to some of the world's most renowned performers, this stunning natural amphitheater has welcomed everyone from The Beatles to U2 for unforgettable performances against a backdrop of red sandstone cliffs. With plenty of trails perfect for hiking or horseback riding, you'll find plenty to enjoy in this unique park!

Location: 18300 W Alameda Pkwy, Morrison, CO 80465-8737

Closest City or Town: Morrison, Colorado

How to Get There: From downtown Denver take I-70 West until you reach exit 259 towards US-HWY 6/Morrison Rd. Turn right onto S Turkey Creek Rd., then turn left onto W Alameda Parkway.

GPS Coordinates: 39.6664666° N, 105.2048546° W

Best Time to Visit: Summer months are best as temperatures tend to be milder during that season **Pass/Permit/Fees:** Entrance is free; individual attractions may charge fees

Did you Know? The rocks were formed over 290 million years ago through a combination of volcanic activity and sedimentary deposition.

Website: http://www.theredrocksamphitheater.com/

MOSCA

Great Sand Dunes National Park

Experience a unique world of endless sand dunes at Great Sand Dunes National Park, located in Mosca, Colorado. Take a hike up the tallest dune in North America and marvel at the beauty of the San Luis Valley. With plenty of trails to explore, this is an excellent place to hike and backpacking or just relaxing with views of snow-capped mountains on one side and golden sands on the other!

Location: 11999 State Highway 150, Mosca, CO 81146-9798

Closest City or Town: Mosca, Colorado

How to Get There: From Alamosa take US-160 E until you reach CO-150 N/Center Ave., turn right onto CO-150 N/CO Rd 350, and follow it until you reach the park entrance.

GPS Coordinates: 37.7440955° N, 105.5069064° W

Best Time to Visit: Summer months are the best time for visiting as temperatures tend to be milder during that season

Pass/Permit/Fees: Entrance fees vary depending on activities ($10-$20). Please visit their website for more details.

Did you Know? The sand is made of quartz and feldspar grains sculpted by wind and water over thousands of years!

Website: http://www.nps.gov/grsa/index.htm

NATHROP

Mt Princeton Hot Springs Stables

Head out into the beautiful Sangre de Cristo mountains with Mt Princeton Hot Springs Stables. Located in Nathrop, Colorado, this is your ideal spot for horseback riding with magnificent views of the Rockies and the Arkansas Valley. Explore rugged trails along mountain streams and pass by meadows lush with pine trees!

Location: 14582 County Road 162, Nathrop, CO 81236-7705

Closest City or Town: Nathrop, Colorado

How to Get There: From Buena Vista take US-285 S until you reach CR 162/Mt Princeton Rd., turn right onto CR162 and follow it until you reach the stables entrance.

GPS Coordinates: 38.740059° N, 106.135409° W

Best Time to Visit: Spring or summer months are best as temperatures tend to be milder during that season

Pass/Permit/Fees: Costs vary depending on the type of riding and the number of people. Please visit their website for more details.

Did you Know? The stables offer an amazing experience for all levels of riders, from beginner to experienced!

Website: http://coloradotrailrides.com/

OURAY

Box Canyon Waterfall & Park

Explore numerous trails and gorgeous waterfalls at Box Canyon Waterfall & Park in Ouray, Colorado. This scenic park offers plenty of opportunities to marvel at nature's beauty, from cascading waterfalls and lush vegetation to rocky outcroppings perfect for climbing. For a truly unique experience, camp under the starry desert sky!

Location: Box Canyon Rd., Ouray, CO 81427-0001

Closest City or Town: Ouray, Colorado

How to Get There: From Ridgway take US-550 N until you reach 4th Ave., turn right onto 4th Ave, and follow it until you reach Box Canyon Rd., turn right onto Box Canyon Rd, and follow it until you reach the park entrance.

GPS Coordinates: 38.0173043° N, 107.676068° W

Best Time to Visit: Spring or summer months are best as temperatures tend to be milder during that season

Pass/Permit/Fees: Entrance is free; individual attractions may charge fees

Did you Know? The park offers a scenic box canyon drive, perfect for a relaxing ride through the canyons!

Website:https://www.ouraycolorado.com/directory/outdoor/parks/54-box-canyon-waterfall-park

Yankee Boy Basin

Discover the wild beauty of Yankee Boy Basin, a high-altitude alpine meadow located in the majestic San Juan Mountains. Hike or drive up to an elevation of 12,400 feet and explore this stunning scenery—from lush wildflowers to snow-capped peaks. Enjoy breathtaking views and snap pictures of the sprawling landscape for an unforgettable adventure!

Location: X6WC+HX Ridgway, Colorado

Closest City or Town: Ridgway, Colorado

How to Get There: Take N Main St/CR 5 toward CR 24 until you reach County Rd 35. Turn left onto CR35 then follow it towards US 550 S/Uncompahgre River Rd until you reach County Rd 34 (Yankee Girl Mine Road). Turn right onto CR34 and continue for about 5 miles to the trailhead parking lot.

GPS Coordinates: 37.9964375° N, 107.7775625° W

Best Time to Visit: Summer months are the best time for visiting as temperatures tend to be milder during that season

Pass/Permit/Fees: No entrance fees are required but a 4x4 vehicle is recommended when driving on the mountain roads.

Did you Know? Yankee Boy Basin is home to over 140 wildflower species!

Website: http://soajeep.com/

Bachelor Syracuse Mine Tour

Go on an unforgettable underground adventure with the Bachelor Syracuse Mine Tour in Ouray, Colorado. Explore the depths of this abandoned silver mine and discover its fascinating history—from tales of tragedy and success to stories about the brave miners who worked here for decades. The tour is family-friendly and features a knowledgeable guide, lighted walkways, educational experiences, and plenty of surprises along the way.

Location: 95 Gold Mountain Trail, Ouray, CO 81427

Closest City or Town: Ouray, Colorado

How to Get There: Follow US-550 S/Million Dollar Highway until you reach Gold Mountain Trail. Turn right onto Gold Mountain Trail and follow it to get to the mine tour parking lot.

GPS Coordinates: 38.0593537° N, 107.6785879° W

Best Time to Visit: The mine tour is available year-round so visit at any time of the year!

Pass/Permit/Fees: Entrance fees vary depending on the type of tour ($9-$25). Please visit their website for more details.

Did you Know? Bachelor Syracuse Mine was once one of the most prosperous mines in Colorado with over $4 million worth of silver extracted!

Website: http://www.bachelorsyracusemine.com/

Ouray Alchemist Museum

Experience the art and science of herbal medicine at Ouray Alchemist Museum. Located in the charming mining town of Ouray, Colorado, this unique museum offers visitors a chance to explore natural remedies and discover the healing properties of herbs from around the world. Learn about centuries-old traditional remedies for common ailments and explore a wide variety of plants that have been used for medical purposes over the years.

Location: 533 Main Street, Ouray, CO 81427

Closest City or Town: Ouray, Colorado

How to Get There: Take US-550 S/Million Dollar Highway until you reach Main Street. Turn right onto Main St and follow it to get to the museum parking lot.

GPS Coordinates: 38.0222122° N, 107.6711383° W

Best Time to Visit: Summer months are the best time for visiting as temperatures tend to be milder during that season

Pass/Permit/Fees: Entrance fees are $8 per person (ages 12+) and $5 per child (ages 4-11).

Did you Know? The Museum is run by a family who have been practicing herbal medicine for generations!

Website: http://ourayalchemist.com/

Perimeter Trail

Take a scenic stroll along the Perimeter Trail located in Ouray, Colorado. This easy-to-moderate hiking trail offers stunning views of the town and its surrounding mountains. Enjoy a peaceful walk through the juniper and pine forests and marvel at the cascading waterfalls while you take in breathtaking panoramic views of the San Juan Mountains.

Location: 1230 Main St, Ouray, CO 81427

Closest City or Town: Ouray, Colorado

How to Get There: Take US-550 S/Million Dollar Highway until you reach Main Street. Turn right onto Main St and follow it towards Rotary Park to get to the trailhead parking lot.

GPS Coordinates: 38.0295237° N, 107.6728413° W

Best Time to Visit: Summer months are the best time for visiting as temperatures tend to be milder during that season

Pass/Permit/Fees: No entrance fees are required.

Did you Know? The trail is part of the larger San Juan Skyway Scenic Byway, which was designated a National Scenic Byway in 1989!

Website: http://www.ouraycolorado.com/Hiking

PAGOSA SPRINGS

Treasure Falls

Get ready for a breathtaking experience at Treasure Falls, a spectacular waterfall located in Pagosa Springs, Colorado. Hike along the trails of the San Juan National Forest to reach this natural wonder and marvel at its beauty as you take in the grand views of the surrounding mountains. For an extra adventure, warm up with a campfire under the starry night sky!

Location: C4VF+34 Pagosa Springs, Colorado

Closest City or Town: Pagosa Springs, Colorado

How to Get There: Located near U.S Highway 160 E.

GPS coordinates are 37.4426875° N, 106.8771875° W.

Best Time to Visit: Summertime is best for exploring comfortably

Pass/Permit/Fees: No fees are required unless camping overnight – please visit their website for more details

Did you Know? The falls cascade from 60 feet above into two pools below - truly a sight to behold!

Website: http://pagosa.com/pagosa-hiking

PHIPPSBURG

Wolf Creek Ski Resort

Enjoy some winter fun at Wolf Creek Ski Resort – one of North America's best powder skiing destinations! From beginner slopes to expert runs that will challenge even the most advanced skiers, Wolf Creek has it all. The resort also offers snowshoeing, sledding, and tubing, making it a great spot for family fun.

Location: Top of Wolf Creek Pass U.S. Hwy 160 E, Pagosa Springs, CO 81147

Closest City or Town: Pagosa Springs, Colorado

How to Get There: Located just off US Highway 160 East

GPS Coordinates are 37.2669486° N, 107.0546248° W

Best Time to Visit: Best time for skiing is between mid-December to mid-April

Pass/Permit/Fees: Entrance fees vary depending on the activity – please visit their website for more details

Did you Know? Wolf Creek is the snowiest ski resort in Colorado with a whopping average of 459 inches of snow a year!

Website: http://www.wolfcreekski.com/

Snow Buddy Dog Sled Tours

Climb aboard for an unforgettable sledding experience with Snow Buddy Dog Sled Tours! Located near Chapman Reservoir, this adventure takes you through breathtaking landscapes as mushers guide their teams of Alaskan huskies around the snowy terrain. Get ready for a truly unique and memorable ride like no other!

Location: Chapman Reservoir Dunkley, CO 81639

Closest City or Town: Grand Junction, Colorado (just a short drive away)

How to Get There: Located near Highway 50 & US 87 E, follow the signs to Chapman Reservoir

GPS Coordinates are 40.1872848° N, 107.0878924° W

Best Time to Visit: Wintertime is best for dog sledding as there's more snow on the ground

Pass/Permit/Fees: Entrance fees vary depending on the activity – please visit their website for more details

Did you Know? Snow Buddy Dog Sled Tours also offers a variety of other activities such as snowshoeing and cross-country skiing!

Website: http://www.snowbuddydogsledtours.com/

RIFLE

Rifle Falls

Take a journey to Rifle Falls State Park for an awe-inspiring experience. Enjoy the sights of the triple waterfall, all cascading from 70 feet above into the bubbling creek below. Check out the nearby caves and hike through scenic trails surrounded by lush foliage.

Location: 5775 Highway 325 Rifle Falls State Park, Rifle, CO 81650-9026

Closest City or Town: The town of Rifle is just over 10 miles away

How to Get There: Located near Highway 325

GPS Coordinates are 39.6742208° N, 107.699228° W

Best Time to Visit: Springtime is best for comfortable weather and plenty of outdoor activities

Pass/Permit/Fees: Entrance fees vary depending on the activity – please visit their website for more details

Did you Know? Rifle Falls State Park is home to rare species of bats, such as Townsend's Big-Eared Bat and Pallid Bat!

Website: https://www.colorado.com/state-parks/rifle-falls-state-park

RYE

Bishop Castle

Explore the breathtaking Bishop Castle, a one-man wonder crafted entirely by Jim Bishop over five decades. Located in the San Isabel National Forest of Rye, Colorado, visitors can marvel at the grand stone towers and turrets that soar above. Inside are colorful stained glass windows and ceilings spanning three stories high! Climb to the top for panoramic views of the surrounding wilderness or explore the ancient armor sculptures dotted around the grounds.

Location: 12705 State Highway 165 San Isabel National Forest, Rye, CO 81069-8634

Closest City or Town: Rye, Colorado (located within the forest)

How to Get There: From downtown Rye head south on US-285 S/US-85 S until you reach County Rd 115. Turn left onto County Rd 115 until you reach County Rd 165 and follow that road for several miles to find Bishop Castle.

GPS Coordinates: 38.0613945° N, 105.0944001° W

Best Time to Visit: Summer months are best as temperatures tend to be milder.

Pass/Permit/Fees: Entrance to the castle is free, but donations are encouraged.

Did you Know? Jim Bishop built the entire structure himself, using only a pickaxe and wheelbarrow!

Website: https://www.bishopcastle.org/

SNOWMASS VILLAGE

Aspen Snowmass

Experience the ultimate adventure at Aspen Snowmass! Located in Snowmass Village, Colorado, this ski resort offers world-class skiing and snowboarding on four different mountains - Aspen Mountain, Aspen Highlands, Buttermilk, and Snowmass. Enjoy some of the best powder in the Rockies with over 5300 acres of varied terrain for all levels. When you're done hitting the slopes take time to relax and explore the vibrant downtown area with its eclectic restaurants and shops.

Location: 130 Kearns Rd, Snowmass Village, CO 81615

Closest City or Town: Snowmass Village (located within the resort)

How to Get There: From downtown Aspen take CO-82 E/E Main St until you reach Snowmass Mall Rd. Turn right onto Snowmass Mall Rd and follow it until you see signs for Aspen Snowmass Entrance.

GPS Coordinates: 39.2114188° N, 106.9475277° W

Best Time to Visit: Winter months are best as the resort is open from November to April each year.

Pass/Permit/Fees: All-day lift tickets cost $154 on peak days and $119 on non-peak days. Please refer to their website for more information.

Did you Know? Aspen Snowmass is one of the most popular ski resorts in North America!

Website: http://www.aspensnowmass.com/our-mountains/snowmass

STEAMBOAT SPRINGS

Steamboat Snowmobile Tours

Experience the wild beauty of the Rockies with Steamboat Snowmobile Tours! Located near Steamboat Springs, Colorado, this tour company offers guided snowmobiling around the stunning Routt National Forest and nearby mountain trails. Race along snowy paths and admire gorgeous views of the Yampa Valley while you drive. At night you can add an extra element of adventure by camping under the starry desert sky!

Location: 31749 Forest Rd 302, Steamboat Springs, CO 80487

Closest City or Town: Steamboat Springs (located within the forest)

How to Get There: From downtown take US-40 W until you reach County Rd 62. Turn right onto County Rd 62 and follow it until you reach Forest Rd 302.

GPS Coordinates: 40.3863679° N, 106.6636025° W

Best Time to Visit: Winter months are best as snowmobiling is only offered from December to March each year.

Pass/Permit/Fees: Prices for a single-day tour cost $225 per person and include all necessary equipment rental. Please refer to their website for more information.

Did you Know? Steamboat Snowmobile Tours offers the largest fleet of Polaris snowmobiles in the area!

Website: http://steamboatsnowmobile.com/

Saddleback Ranch

Experience the beauty of a western dude ranch at Saddleback Ranch. Located in Steamboat Springs, Colorado, this family-friendly destination is perfect for outdoor adventurers who want to explore nature on horseback. Enjoy spectacular views while riding through a scenic valley of rolling hills and open meadows or take advantage of the opportunity to camp under the starry night sky. With its stunning mountain backdrop and idyllic setting, Saddleback Ranch will be an unforgettable experience you'll never forget!

Location: 37500 County Road 179, Steamboat Springs, CO 80487-9501

Closest City or Town: Steamboat Springs, Colorado

How to Get There: From downtown Steamboat Springs, take County Road 16 and then turn onto County Road 179 to reach the ranch.

GPS Coordinates: 40.4612328° N, 106.9879056° W

Best Time to Visit: Summer months are best for enjoying all that Saddleback has to offer **Pass/Permit/Fees:** Prices vary depending on activities - please visit their website for more details **Did you Know?** The ranch offers lessons in roping and Western riding styles suitable for all skill levels!

Website: http://www.saddlebackranch.net/

Grizzle-T Dog & Sled Works

Discover the beautiful landscapes of Colorado like never before with Grizzle-T Dog & Sled Works! Located in Steamboat Springs, this adventure tour will take you on an unforgettable ride through the wilderness with beautiful views of the Yampa Valley. Sit back and relax as skilled mushers lead a team of friendly sled dogs through scenic trails for a truly unique experience. Whether you are looking to explore nature or just have fun, Grizzle-T Dog & Sled Works has something for everyone!

Location: HC 66 Box 39, Steamboat Springs, CO 80487

Closest City or Town: Steamboat Springs, Colorado

How to Get There: From downtown Steamboat Springs take County Road 37 until you reach Routt County Road 33. Turn onto Grizzly Creek Rd., then turn right when you reach Rollingstone Dr. and follow it until you reach Grizzle-T Dog & Sled Works.

GPS Coordinates: 40.4849769° N, 106.8317158° W

Best Time to Visit: Winter months are best for sledding tours at the ranch **Pass/Permit/Fees:** Prices vary depending on activities - please visit their website for more details

Did you Know? Grizzly-T has been in operation since 1988 and offers different tour routes to pick from!

Website: http://steamboatdogsledding.com/

Fish Creek Falls

Take a break from your daily routine and enjoy the beauty of Colorado's outdoors with a visit to Fish Creek Falls! Located in Steamboat Springs, this breathtaking waterfall is a popular destination for hikers and nature lovers. Stroll along the scenic trails, breathe in the fresh mountain air, and marvel at the majestic falls cascading down from a rocky ledge. Whether you are looking to explore nature or just have some fun with friends and family, Fish Creek Falls is sure to be an experience you won't forget!

Location: Fish Creek Falls Road County Road 32, Steamboat Springs, CO 80477

Closest City or Town: Steamboat Springs, Colorado

How to Get There: From downtown Steamboat Springs head east on Lincoln Ave. until you reach US-40 E then take County Rd 33 until you reach Fish Creek Falls Rd. Turn right onto the road and follow it until you reach the falls.

GPS Coordinates: 40.4833316° N, 106.8158464° W

Best Time to Visit: Summer months provide optimal foliage visibility
Pass/Permit/Fees: Free entrance

Did you Know? The area around Fish Creek Falls is also known for its abundant wildlife, including deer, elk, bear, and other species!

Website:
http://www.fs.usda.gov/recarea/mbr/recreation/hiking/recarea/?recid=22746&actid=50

Steamboat Ski Resort

Experience the magic of winter at Steamboat Ski Resort! Located in Steamboat Springs, this winter wonderland is a popular destination for skiers and snowboarders alike. From beginner to expert trails, the resort offers something for everyone. Enjoy breathtaking views of the Yampa Valley while conquering challenging alpine terrain or take a break from the slopes with a gondola ride up Mt. Werner. Whether you are looking to have some fun on the powdery slopes or just relax in an idyllic setting, Steamboat Ski Resort will be an unforgettable experience.

Location: 2305 Mount Werner Cir, Steamboat Springs, CO 80487-9023

Closest City or Town: Steamboat Springs, Colorado

How to Get There: From downtown Steamboat Springs head east on Lincoln Ave and then turn onto Mt. Werner Rd. Follow the road until you reach Steamboat Ski Resort

GPS Coordinates: 40.4570979° N, 106.8044718° W

Best Time to Visit: The ski season typically runs from November through April **Pass/Permit/Fees:** Prices vary depending on activities - please visit their website for more details

Did you Know? The resort has over 165 trails spanning 2,965 acres across 6 mountains!

Website: http://www.steamboat.com/

Yampa River Botanic Park

Explore the stunning beauty of the Yampa Valley at the Yampa River Botanic Park. Located in Steamboat Springs, Colorado, this peaceful refuge offers a chance to connect with nature and discover native plants and wildlife in harmony. Enjoy walking along meandering riverbeds or take a leisurely stroll through winding paths lined by tall cottonwood trees. Unwind under the starry night sky while camping at one of its many designated sites for an unforgettable experience!

Location: 1000 Pamela Lane, Steamboat Springs, CO 80487

Closest City or Town: Steamboat Springs, Colorado

How to Get There: Take Emerld Parkway from S. Lincoln Avenue and follow the Yampa River Botanic Park signs.

GPS Coordinates: 40.4697475° N, 106.8289787° W

Best Time to Visit: Summer months are ideal for camping in the park while spring is best for hiking as wildflowers bloom throughout the valley.

Pass/Permit/Fees: Entry and campsites must be reserved online with applicable fees charged per night ($15-$25).

Did you Know? Built on land that was once part of a Ute Indian Reservation, the Yampa River Botanic Park is rich with history and culture.

Website: http://www.yampariverbotanicpark.org/

Steamboat Gondola

See Steamboat Springs from a new perspective with a unique experience aboard the Steamboat Gondola. Glide up to the top of Mount Werner and take in breathtaking views of the Yampa Valley below. Take in the beauty of alpine meadows, glittering lakes, and snow-capped peaks as you soar into the sky!

Location: 2305 Mount Werner Cir, Steamboat Springs, CO 80487-9023

Closest City or Town: Steamboat Springs, Colorado

How to Get There: Drive along Mt Werner Rd until you reach the gondola entrance at 2305 Mt. Werner Circle.

GPS Coordinates: 40.4570979° N, 106.8044718° W

Best Time to Visit: Summer months offer the best views with warmer temperatures, while winter provides spectacular skiing opportunities.

Pass/Permit/Fees: Tickets are required for gondola rides and fees vary depending on activity ($10-$42).

Did you Know? The Steamboat Gondola is the longest free-standing lift in North America!

Website: http://www.steamboat.com/plan-vacation/activities/details/index.aspx?id=53#steamboat-gondola

Yampa River Core Trail

Take a peaceful walk along one of Colorado's premier trails at Yampa River Core Trail. This tranquil path extends from Rabbit Ears Pass all the way to the historic town of Oak Creek. Enjoy diverse wildlife and picturesque views of the Yampa Valley while exploring its many hidden gems.

Location: 936282004, Steamboat Springs, CO 80487

Closest City or Town: Steamboat Springs, Colorado

How to Get There: Drive along US-40 heading east towards Rabbit Ears Pass until you reach the trailhead parking lot.

GPS Coordinates: 40.4849769° N, 106.8317158° W

Best Time to Visit: April through October offer mild temperatures and lush vegetation with stunning autumn colors in November.

Pass/Permit/Fees: The trail is free and open to the public year-round.

Did you Know? Yampa Core Trail was once used by Ute Indians for hunting, and the historic trail is still visible today!

Website: http://steamboatsprings.net/index.aspx?nid=307

TELLURIDE

Telluride Mountain Village Gondola

Experience a one-of-a-kind journey with Telluride Mountain Village Gondola! Make your way up to the majestic San Sophia Ridge where you can explore alpine meadows and enjoy breathtaking views of the Rocky Mountains. Take in the sights and sounds of vibrant wildflowers while taking a leisurely ride along this scenic route!

Location: 455 Mountain Village Blvd, Telluride, CO 81435-9459

Closest City or Town: Telluride, Colorado

How to Get There: Take the highway from Ridgway towards Telluride and follow Village Drive until you reach the Mountain Village Gondola entrance.

GPS Coordinates: 37.9334780° N, 107.8540365° W

Best Time to Visit: Spring through summer months offer bright colors of wildflowers in bloom while winter is best for skiing and snowboarding opportunities.

Pass/Permit/Fees: Tickets are required for gondola rides with fees varying on activity ($3-$50).

Did you Know? The Telluride Golf Course lies at the top of the gondola, offering a one-of-a-kind golfing experience with breathtaking views of San Sophia Ridge!

Website: http://www.visittelluride.com/telluride-gondola

Bear Creek Falls

Located in Telluride, Colorado, Bear Creek Falls is the perfect spot for nature lovers. Trek along the trails and enjoy breathtaking views of cascading waterfalls or take a dip in one of the many pools. Make sure to bring your camping gear so you can sleep under the starry night sky for an unforgettable experience!

Location: Bear Creek Falls Trail, Telluride, CO 81435

COLORADO BUCKET LIST

Closest Town: Telluride, CO (just a short drive away)

How to Get There: From downtown Telluride head west on W Colorado Ave until you reach S Davis St/CO-145. Turn left onto S Frontage Rd E and follow it until you get to Booth Lake Rd before making a right turn into the parking lot area.

GPS Coordinates: 37.9079486° N, 107.8112197° W

Best Time to Visit: The best time for visiting is during late spring and early summer when temperatures are milder yet still comfortable

Pass/Permit/Fees: Entrance fees vary depending on activities ($10-$20). Please visit their website for more details.

Did you Know? This area was once used by local miners as pasture land and some believe that bears were named after it as a result.

Website: http://www.visittelluride.com/activity/bear-creek-trail

VAIL

Betty Ford Alpine Gardens

Visit the Betty Ford Alpine Gardens in Vail, Colorado, and explore seven acres of lush gardens showcasing plants from alpine tundra to wildflower meadows. Take a leisurely stroll along the nature trails and admire the breathtaking views of the mountain peaks or join one of their educational events such as guided tours or talks with botanists. This is an ideal spot for gardeners who want to get up close to nature!

Location: 522 S Frontage Rd E, Vail, CO 81657-4550

Closest Town: Vail, Colorado (just a short drive away)

How to Get There: From downtown Vail take I-70 E until you reach S Frontage Rd E/Exit 176. Turn left onto S Frontage Rd E and follow it until you get to the Betty Ford Alpine Gardens entrance.

GPS Coordinates: 39.6416465° N, 106.3676753° W

Best Time to Visit: The best time for visiting is during late spring when the wildflowers are in full bloom and temperatures are milder yet still comfortable

Pass/Permit/Fees: Entrance fees vary depending on activities ($10-$20). Please visit their website for more details.

Did you Know? There is a Wildflower Festival held each year in late June showcasing hundreds of different plant species found in Colorado's Rocky Mountains. It's a great way to learn more about Colorado's unique flora and fauna.

Website: http://bettyfordalpinegardens.org/

Vail Valley

Visit the Vail Valley, located in the heart of Colorado's Rocky Mountains, for a truly unforgettable experience. With its serene rivers, lush meadows, and tranquil lakes, nature lovers will be in awe of this stunning landscape. From rafting trips to horseback riding to simply strolling along the trails, there is something here for everyone!

Location: 241 S Frontage Rd W #8150, Vail, CO 81657

Closest Town: Vail, Colorado (just a short drive away)

How to Get There: From downtown Vail take I-70 E until you reach S Frontage Rd W/Exit 176. Turn left onto S Frontage Rd W and follow it until you get to the entrance of the Vail Valley.

GPS Coordinates: 39.6438623° N, 106.3794565° W

Best Time to Visit: The best time for visiting is during summer when temperatures are milder yet still comfortable

Pass/Permit/Fees: Entrance fees may apply depending on activities ($10-$20). Please visit their website for more details.

Did you Know? This area is home to many species of wildlife including elk, moose, deer, and mountain lions making it a great spot for wildlife enthusiasts.

Website: http://www.visitvailvalley.com/

Booth Falls Trail

Experience the beauty of Colorado's Rocky Mountains from Booth Falls Trail in Vail, Colorado. This five-mile trail takes you through forests and meadows filled with wildflowers while offering you stunning views of cascading waterfalls. Enjoy a picnic lunch next to one of the many peaceful lakes or go fishing in the crystal clear waters - it is the perfect destination for outdoor adventurers!

Location: 3035 Booth Falls Rd, Vail, CO 81657

Closest Town: Vail, Colorado (just a short drive away)

How to Get There: From downtown Vail take I-70 E until you reach S Frontage Rd W/Exit 176. Turn left onto S Frontage Rd W and follow it until you get to the Booth Falls Trailhead.

GPS Coordinates: 39.6502544° N, 106.3210634° W

Best Time to Visit: The best time for visiting is during summer when temperatures are milder yet still comfortable

Pass/Permit/Fees: Entrance fees may apply depending on activities ($10-$20). Please visit their website for more details.

Did you Know? This area is home to numerous species of wildlife including marmots, black bears, elk, and mountain goats making it a great spot for wildlife enthusiasts.

Website:
https://www.fs.usda.gov/recarea/whiteriver/recreation/hiking/recarea/?recid=12212&actid=50

WESTMINSTER

Butterfly Pavilion

Located in Westminster, Colorado, the Butterfly Pavilion lets visitors get up close and personal with thousands of beautiful butterflies from around the world. You can even feed them! An insect zoo provides a unique opportunity to explore and learn about arthropods like bees, millipedes, and tarantulas. There's also a lush rainforest full of exotic plants that provide a natural habitat for the butterflies to flutter around in. Enjoy an educational experience that will leave you mesmerized by these amazing creatures.

Location: 6252 W 104th Ave, Westminster, CO 80020-4107

Closest City or Town: Westminster, Colorado (just minutes away)

How to Get There: Take US-36 W/Church Ranch Blvd towards 104th Avenue until you reach West 104th Ave., then turn left at this intersection to reach the pavilion entrance.

GPS Coordinates: 39.887153° N, 105.066427° W

Best Time to Visit: The best time for visiting is early spring when most species are out flying around in their natural habitats.

Pass/Permit/Fees: The admission fee varies depending on age ($5-$15). For more details please visit their website.

Did you Know? The Butterfly Pavilion houses over 50 different species of butterflies, making it one of the largest collections in North America.

Website: http://www.butterflies.org/

WINTER PARK

Grand Adventures

Discover adventure and thrills at Grand Adventures! Located on US Highway 40 in Winter Park, Colorado, you can experience some of the best winter activities in the state with snowmobile tours, snowshoe hikes, and skiing and tubing adventures. Or if you're looking for a summer activity there are great mountain biking trails, 4x4 off-roading trails, and even ATV rentals available so you can explore to your heart's content. With breathtaking views of the Arapaho National Forest and the Rocky Mountains - this is the perfect spot for those who love nature and outdoor sports!

Location: 78311 US HWY 40 Ste 100, Winter Park, CO 80482

Closest City or Town: Winter Park, Colorado (just steps away)

How to Get There: Take US-40 W/Grand Ave. until you reach the intersection with Colorado Hwy 821 (Tabor Rd). Then turn left onto Co Rd 83 and follow it until you reach Grand Adventures entrance.

GPS Coordinates: 39.9266236° N, 105.7875681° W

Best Time to Visit: The best time for visiting is late winter when snowfall provides ideal conditions for skiing and other winter activities.

Pass/Permit/Fees: Admission fees vary depending on the activity ($20-$65). Please visit their website for more details.

Did you Know?: Grand Adventures has over 150 miles of trails to explore, making it one of the largest recreation areas in Colorado.

Website: http://www.grandadventures.com/

Map

We have devised an interactive map that includes all destinations described in the book.

Upon scanning a provided QR code, a link will be sent to your email, allowing you access to this unique digital feature.

This map is both detailed and user-friendly, marking every location described within the pages of the book. It provides accurate addresses and GPS coordinates for each location, coupled with direct links to the websites of these stunning destinations.

Once you receive your email link and access the interactive map, you'll have an immediate and comprehensive overview of each site's location. This invaluable tool simplifies trip planning and navigation, making it a crucial asset for both first-time visitors and seasoned explorers of Colorado.

Scan the following QR or type in the provided link to receive it:

https://jo.my/cobucketlistform

You will receive an email with links to access the Interactive Map. If you do not see our email, please look for it in spam or another section of your inbox.

In case you have any problems, you can write us at TravelBucketList@becrepress.com

Made in the USA
Las Vegas, NV
23 October 2024